Tamsin

God bless your family and in
all that you do!

Kathy

"It is the stories of those who have radically followed Jesus that stir my heart and ignite a deeper faith for what God has called me to. It is in the mountains and the valleys, the challenges and the victories and the tears and the celebrations that I see the faithfulness and goodness of God on display. God brought Kris and Kathy Vallotton into my life when I was a young man. Their lives and the stories they told helped shape me into who I am, and they are still with me today. I know that *The Good, the God and the Ugly* will do the same for you. This book will challenge and inspire you to live a radical life of faith and draw you into a deeper relationship with God."

Banning Liebscher, founder and pastor, Jesus Culture; author, *The Three-Mile Walk: The Courage You Need to Live the Life God Wants for You*

"One of the greatest gifts has been my connection to the Vallotton family. There has never been a question too personal or response too reserved. In *The Good, the God and the Ugly*, Kathy beautifully shares details of living an abundant life despite circumstances. Whether you are a newlywed or have a seasoned family, get your hands on this book!"

Havilah Cunnington, founder, Truth to Table

"Kathy and her husband, Kris, live in an environment very different from ours, but they have chosen a life no less dependent on faith—and they have proven countless times that they are the kind of friends you can rely on, no matter what. Their story has been a pure blessing to us."

Heidi G. Baker, Ph.D., co-founder and executive chairman of the board, Iris Global

"We have an unconventional love story about to be revealed in these pages! Kris and Kathy Vallotton know how to create epic stories out of life. Prepare to hear things you had no idea could even happen, let alone become normal occurrences. This perfectly titled book, *The Good, the God and the Ugly*, will keep you laughing, shocked, amazed and hope-filled while you can't put it down. I am happy to congratulate and endorse my good friend Kathy Vallotton for this beautiful capture of history with Kris."

Danny Silk, president, Loving On Purpose;
author, *Keep Your Love On* and more

"*The Good, the God and the Ugly* paints a real-life, behind-the-scenes look at one of the most powerful ministry families in America. Kathy writes with a vulnerability and frankness that creates a fun and insightful read tastefully seasoned with life-changing principles."

Dan McCollam, co-founder, Bethel School of the Prophets
and The Prophetic Company; author, *Bending Time*,
Finding Lost Things, God Vibrations and more

"This book is a compelling read. Kathy's stories transported me to an oasis where my faith rose, peace was restored, I laughed out loud and all became well again with my soul. An undeniable testimony that 'the God of peace will be with you.'"

Keri Warden Owen, iCoaching with Horses

THE GOOD,
THE GOD
AND
THE UGLY

THE GOOD,
THE GOD
AND
THE UGLY

THE INSIDE STORY OF A
SUPERNATURAL FAMILY

KATHY VALLOTTON

Chosen

a division of Baker Publishing Group
Minneapolis, Minnesota

© 2021 by Kathy Vallotton

Published by Chosen Books
11400 Hampshire Avenue South
Bloomington, Minnesota 55438
www.chosenbooks.com

Chosen Books is a division of
Baker Publishing Group, Grand Rapids, Michigan

Printed in the United States of America

Library of Congress Control Number: 2020949493

ISBN 978-0-8007-6187-5 (cloth)
ISBN 978-0-8007-6188-2 (paperback)
ISBN 978-1-4934-3007-9 (ebook)

Cover design by LOOK Design Studio

21 22 23 24 25 26 27   7 6 5 4 3 2 1

I dedicate this book to my husband, Kris,
to my family and to those whom I have done life with.
For without all of you,
my life would be pretty boring.

CONTENTS

FOREWORD

We first met Kris and Kathy in the small mountain community of Weaverville in Northern California. We had moved there to pastor a church by the name of Mountain Chapel. Kris was just recovering from a nervous breakdown, yet he still managed to have more zeal and passion for the Lord than just about anyone else. Both of them had a hunger for God that caused them to stand out significantly. And what impacted us the most was their tireless effort to serve wherever needed. In fact, the strength of their service was that no job was too small, nor did they need micromanagement to complete a task. They would always figure out a way to accomplish their assignment—a pastor's dream.

At one point, our only pianist moved out of the area. We had no one to help with worship, which was a high priority in both our personal lives and our corporate gatherings. One day Kathy told me she had taken piano lessons as a child and would be happy to help me out. She asked me to give her one song to learn that week. I did. The following Sunday we sang that one song. The next week she learned a second one, and so on, until she could play for an entire worship service of 45 minutes to an hour. Kathy eventually became the anchor to a thriving worship ministry with many members. Kathy is a true worshiper, a genuine servant of God.

As our friendship grew, our families spent more and more time together. In fact, you could say we raised our kids together and pursued more of the things of the Lord. We even lived together for a season, with five kids, four adults and one pet rat in our rather small home, while they built their house. On more than one occasion we emptied our pockets and scoured the house for spare change until we had enough money to buy a half gallon of ice cream, which our families would enjoy together that evening. They have been friends in life and partners in ministry now for over forty years.

When my dad pastored Bethel here in Redding, California, he taught me many invaluable lessons. One of those was when he once interviewed many potential prospects to take on the pastoral position of the music/worship director. He chose someone who didn't have all the skills needed for the position. He then shared with us that while the man he chose didn't have all the qualifications needed for the job, he had the same heart that we did. "Skills can be taught," he would say; it was the heart that mattered. Kris and Kathy Vallotton have carried a remarkable heart of love and loyalty for both God and people. The beauty of this reality is manifest on every page of this book.

The Good, the God and the Ugly is a very inspirational book. Perhaps we should call it an adventure in print. Kathy shares about the fun, hilarious, yet challenging journey of the Vallotton family. She shares a perspective on the development of a prophet that only a wife could give. Kathy weaves together a teenage love story with parenting adventures, the roller coaster of business ownership and the beautiful journey of one woman's complete devotion to God. Her stories are poignant and hilarious (just try to read the story of Kris learning to downhill ski without laughing). As such, they are filled with wisdom. She is very honest about their moments of crisis and shares with delight the testimonies of incredible breakthrough, highlighting the lessons gleaned from a life dedicated to serving God.

We have worked together for the majority of our lives, both in Weaverville and now in Redding, and the Vallottons' influence has been integral to every part of Bethel's culture. Kris has the more public ministry. But in our world, Kathy is well-known as the stable support and administrator to this incredible visionary. They are the perfect pair! She's often the one working behind the scenes without whom we would all suffer. She is a source of strength, peace, strategic thinking and joy. Kathy knows her identity in Christ. As a result, she embraces the privilege to serve, enabling those around her to enter their place of significance. She has become a powerful leader in Bethel Church and Bethel School of Supernatural Ministry. She is a spiritual mother to many.

In her final chapter, Kathy speaks about legacy and the Vallottons' desire to impact a future generation they won't be alive to see. We can say, without a doubt, that this passion has helped to set the stage for the profound impact on many generations to come. Their lives have challenged, supported and changed all of us. We are all richer because of their yes to God.

And we are so grateful for their love and their steadfast pursuit of the Father's heart.

If Kris has impacted you in any way, you must read this book. It is vital to see the other side of the story, through the eyes of the one who has done so much to make it all happen. It is unusually inspirational to see how God raised up this couple with international influence through such humble beginnings. Even if you haven't been exposed to Kris's ministry, you should read this book anyway. It will open up for you the joy of the journey, instilling the confidence in God's ability to turn any situation into one that brings Him glory, all while bringing us into a place of greater strength. We believe this book will impart courage into the heart of every person who reads it.

Bill and Beni Johnson, Bethel Church, Redding, California;
authors, *Born for Significance*, *The Way of Life*,
Raising Giant-Killers, *The Mind of God* and more

ACKNOWLEDGMENTS

Kris: God smiled down on me when he blessed me with you. You have been the love of my life and my greatest encourager. I could never imagine my life without you in it. Every day spent with you is a new adventure, one that I am willing to take.

Jaime and Marty: I love you both! You both are such an example of strong leaders in the church. Jaime, thank you for all your encouragement, pushing me forward past my fears of riding my big boy, Dreamer.

Shannon: I love you so much. The inner strength that comes from Jesus lights the path that causes so many people to follow you. Your love for others doesn't go unnoticed. You are one strong woman!

Jason and Lauren: Jay, you have been such an amazing hunting and fishing buddy. Not many moms can say that. I love the fact that you take such an interest in me. It doesn't go unnoticed. Lauren, you are God's gift to our family. Thank you for loving my grandkids and giving us one more!

Gene: Thank you for saying yes to our family! Your love for others is contagious. You are such a gift to me. I love you, son.

Mom and Rhonda: You both are two of the strongest women that I know. Thank you for believing in me and loving me through all those crazy teenage years. I could only imagine the conversations that you and Dad had during my dating years.

My grandkids, Mesha, Micah, Alana, Elijah, Rilie, Evan, Baby Edie, Isaac, Ella and Jackson: Thank you for giving me things to write about! Your stories will go on forever. I am so proud of each one of you. My quiver is full and I am so blessed. I love you all!

Bill and Beni: My life would have looked quite different if it wasn't for you and your family. Thank you for believing in Kris and me, for stepping outside of your comfort level at times and taking the risk that was definitely out of your comfort zone.

ONE

THE DAY I MET YOU

Many waters cannot quench love, nor will rivers overflow it.

SONG OF SOLOMON 8:7

I hardly know life without Kris. I can still remember when we met for the first time. I was camping at Clear Lake, California, with my family, where we had hung out with the same friends every year since the time I was a little girl. I had no clue what was about to happen to my heart! I was floating on a raft, basking in the water, when I suddenly eyed this skinny, good-looking brown-haired guy next to the dock. He was working on a boat with his friend. I spent the next three hours floating on a raft in my bikini, hoping to grab his attention. And although I was only twelve years old, my age had betrayed me. I had hit puberty at eight, so I was already a girl-woman on the hunt for a man. My quiet personality hid my raging desire for male companionship from the outside world. So there I was, fishing for a man, not sure if I had caught his eye, but very sure I was getting burnt to a crisp trying.

I looked up at the dock and could tell that the guys were nearly done with their project. *Wow, he's cute!* I mused. Just then, that good-looking guy glanced over at me and smiled. *Oh my gosh!* My heart froze, and I almost fell off my raft. Then I suddenly realized that I knew his friend from previous years at the camp. His name was Gary. *I'll run into them again,* I said to myself, looking innocent but devising a plot in my heart.

That evening, Gary and his handsome friend came by my campsite. My grandmother greeted them as they introduced themselves.

"Is Kathy here?" Gary asked.

My grandmother glared at them, giving them the evil eye. (Remember, I was only twelve years old.) When I heard their voices, I came blasting out of my tent. I wanted to get to the guys before my grandmother had the chance to boot them out of our camp, because in those days she was a guard dog for my soul.

"Hi, Gary!" I said in the most inviting tone I could muster. "It's been a while since I've seen you. How've you been?"

"Hey, doing great! This is my friend Kris. We're going to take the boat out tomorrow to go skiing. Do you want to come?" Gary inquired.

My heart was racing. I could not believe that they were asking me to join them. "I'd love to go. Let me ask my parents, to make sure it's all right."

"Mom, Dad, I met this guy who came camping with Gary, and they want to take me skiing with them tomorrow. Can I go?" I asked.

"You're pretty young to be out with two strange guys on the lake," my mom warned. The truth is, my mother had fallen in love with my dad when she was eleven years old, so she probably suspected there was more going on in my heart than was evident in my personality.

"Come on, Mom! We won't be gone long. We're just going skiing. I'll be careful!" I pushed back. After some banter back and forth, and a little bargaining, my mom finally said yes.

When morning dawned, I was crazy excited about the day. When I crawled out of my sleeping bag, however, I was writhing in pain. I looked down at my body, and I was cooked beet red! *I am so stupid*, I said to myself. *I shouldn't have been out on that raft for so long. I'll be paying for it today.* Yet truth be known, I was actually more concerned about how I looked than how I felt.

A little while later, the guys came by my campsite to pick me up. They were quite the pair. I am sure they were trying to be on their best behavior, especially in front of my grandmother, who was still giving them "the stare."

"I'm going to go with you guys, but I won't be able to ski. I'm so sunburned that I can hardly move," I confessed.

"You might try some sunscreen or a tarp or something next time," Kris joked. His attention made my heart race! I grabbed my things, and we headed down to the shore.

It was a great day to be on the lake. The water was like glass, and the sun was . . . well, let's just say the sun was not as raging hot as it was the day before. The three of us jumped in the boat, and the vessel took off as if it was captained by three teenagers. We finally found a great spot to ski—still, calm waters with hardly another boat in sight. Gary jumped in the water with his slalom ski. Obviously, he was an experienced skier. A minute later, he grabbed the tow rope and yelled "Hit it!"

Immediately Kris gunned the motor, and Gary popped up out of the water like a pro. He skied around the lake, cutting from side to side as he gracefully jumped the wake of the boat. After about fifteen minutes he signaled he was done, let go of the rope and dropped into the water.

Next, it was Kris's turn. I looked over at him and laughed as he readied himself for the ride. He had on a ski vest, as well as a ski belt. He must have seen me laughing, because he commented on the fact that he couldn't swim and there was no way he was going to go under the water.

No chance of that happening, I thought to myself as I looked at him. Gary came to his rescue, explaining that Kris was just learning how to ski. A guy who couldn't swim, learning to ski for the first time, dressed up like a bobber—I didn't know if I could contain myself. When he jumped into the water, he floated so high that he looked like a buoy. I almost fell overboard trying not to laugh.

Kris held on to the rope as if his life depended on it. His two skis separated as if they were attached to an uncoordinated man who had no control over his limbs. The boat then began to pull him up slowly as Gary shouted instructions at him. Kris planed the water for a few seconds and then crumbled into the lake, dragging his skis behind him until they were finally forced off his feet. They ended up floating several yards away from him. For his next feat, Kris had to swim to the skis and get them back on his feet, all while floating like a bobber from his waist up.

I don't know if I can even find words to describe the scene—a man terrified of the water, trying to get two skis on his feet while spinning around, sometimes facedown as if he were drowning, all while Gary shouted instructions from the bow of the boat. I couldn't handle it anymore! I burst into hysterical laughter, wincing uncontrollably and nearly falling out of the boat because I was in tears from laughing so hard!

> **A guy who couldn't swim, learning to ski for the first time, dressed up like a bobber—I didn't know if I could contain myself.**

This whole scene repeated itself over and over, until finally Kris stood up on his skis with a huge grin on his face as Gary and I cheered him on. Kris had tackled the feat of getting up on the skis, but then once he fell, he was terrified to let go of the rope. There he was, holding on for dear life as he bobbed up and down in the water, with both life preservers holding him up. A few minutes later, he succumbed to the water and let go of the rope. He wanted to try it again, but Gary was pretty done pulling him around the lake like a fisherman trolling for sharks. I was kind of glad Kris was done skiing for the day, too, since my stomach hurt so badly from laughing.

Lost in Time

The next day, Kris came by my campsite and asked my mother if I could go on a motorcycle ride the next morning. "There are lots of logging roads around, so we won't be on the main highway," Kris explained. "Gary and I have already scouted them out, and they're safe for us to ride on."

My grandmother was near, and she was locked into guard dog mode. Just as she was about to make the *No way!* decree, Mom stepped in, pulled rank and told me I could go riding with the guys for an hour.

I woke up the next morning with excitement in my heart. I did not have much in the way of motorcycle attire, but I made sure I was wearing long pants and closed-toe shoes. Soon, Kris and Gary came driving up on their motorcycles. Kris had a brand-new green Honda 100. I thought he looked so amazing on the bike. The fact that I was impressed with a skinny guy sitting on a Honda 100 was a sure sign of my immaturity. Is a Honda 100 even considered a real motorcycle? I don't know. But off we went as I waved to my family on our way out of camp.

Our ride was amazing, and the scenery was beautiful. We rode down dirt roads, forded a creek and zigzagged through the forest on deer trails that went nowhere. Kris was such a gentleman the whole way. When we stopped for a break and checked on the time, we panicked because we had been gone for hours. We quickly climbed back on the bikes and headed back to camp. When we approached the entrance, we noticed a large gathering of people apparently waiting for us.

"That looks like my parents and grandma," I warned. "They don't look very happy. . . . I think I'm in big trouble!"

"Where have you been? Do you know what time it is?" my dad questioned, with my grandmother glaring at the boys, swords shooting out of her eyes.

I tried to get a word in edgewise, but Dad kept going on and on. I finally stopped trying to explain myself and just raised my hands in remorse, confessing, "I'm sorry, Dad. We were having so much fun that I didn't realize how long we had been gone."

> I was worried that Kris would perceive me now as a little girl instead of a mature woman, and he would never want to see me again!

I was embarrassed that my father was scolding me like a twelve-year-old child in front of my two fifteen-year-old high school friends. But more importantly, I was worried that Kris would perceive me now as a little girl instead of a mature woman, and he would never want to see me again!

Walking back to camp, I apologized again to my parents. I honestly understood why they were mad. They had given me permission to be gone for one hour, but we had disappeared for the entire day. Looking back now, I know I would have grounded our girls until they were thirty in that same scenario. That day revealed that although I had the body of a mature woman, my brain still had the underdeveloped frontal cortex of a teen (or preteen, in my case).

Gone Forever?

I only got to spend three days with Kris before he left Clear Lake to go back home, but I could not believe the feelings I was having for him. He was kind and considerate, but most of all, he made me feel like a real woman. And he liked me for who I was. I did not want this to end. I think right there and then, I fell in love with Kris.

"Impossible," you say. I don't think so. I would call it God's divine destiny for my life!

When the day came for Kris to leave camp, I realized I had been dreading this day since the moment we met. Saying good-bye was the hardest thing I had ever done. I had no idea how Kris felt about me, but I sure knew how I felt about him! My heart leapt out of my chest every time I saw Kris, and now I didn't know if I would ever see him again.

When Gary's father told the guys it was time to leave, I watched as Kris and Gary climbed into the car and it started moving slowly down the gravel road. The guys waved good-bye as the car gradually disappeared in the morning sun.

He's really gone! I grieved. I walked slowly back to our campsite, holding back the tears welling up in my eyes. I just needed some time by myself. Looking up, I saw my family eating breakfasr, but I did not feel like talking to anyone. I veered off and headed toward the lake, soon finding myself at the end of the dock, where we used to hang out.

I don't know how many tears dropped into the lake that day, but it was a lot. Deep down inside, I knew that Kris was the right person for me, and I had to see him again. I did not have his phone number or even his address, for that matter, but I did know that somehow, somewhere, we would find each other again.

> **Deep down inside, I knew that Kris was the right person for me, and I had to see him again.**

The rest of the story is quite miraculous. Kris had left a jacket back at his campsite, and I picked it up, determined to return it to him. Once we left Clear Lake and arrived back home, I started looking through the phone book for the name *Vallotton*. I knew that Kris lived in Sunnyvale, California, but I did not know that he had a different last name than his mom and stepfather. Still, I was in luck! There were only a few Vallottons in the Bay Area, and only one of them lived in Sunnyvale.

I dialed the number I found and immediately discovered that I was talking to Kris's grandmother, who lived just a few blocks from him. I told her who I was and that I was trying to return a jacket to Kris and would like his phone number, if she could give it to me. Thankfully, I must have won her over, because I hung up the phone with his number in my hand.

I dialed his number, my heart pounding out of my chest and my mind preparing me for rejection. Kris's mother answered the phone. She was kind and friendly, and her voice was reassuring.

A few seconds later, Kris himself was on the phone. "Hey, Kathy, how are you?" he inquired.

"Good . . . I mean, great . . . yeah, I'm doing great," I replied nervously. "You left your coat at the lake, and I'm . . . well . . . I'm going to be in the area tomorrow, and if it's okay, I can . . . maybe I can bring it to your house if you're going to be home, or something?"

"Great! I'd really appreciate you bringing it to me," Kris replied. "I'll be home all day, so just stop by anytime, Kathy."

My heart was exploding with relief, excitement and joy. "Okay, I'll see you then." When I hung up the phone, I wanted to run around the house ten times while shouting at the top of my lungs, "I love you, Kris Vallotton!" I could hardly contain myself.

> **When I left his house that day, his mother looked him in the eyes and proclaimed, "Now, that's the marrying kind!"**

The next day, I arrived at Kris's house around noon and found myself a little surprised by the low-income neighborhood he lived in. But with his coat in hand and my heart in my throat, I made my way to the front door. His mother greeted me and invited me in as she opened the screen door. Her name was Shirley, and she was beautiful, bubbly and engaging. I could feel my anxiety drain out of my feet as she talked.

A few minutes later, Kris joined us in the kitchen, and I felt excitement fill my heart again. I nervously handed him his coat as we recounted our time at Clear Lake to Shirley. We laughed a bunch, but my parents were waiting for me in the car and I felt pressured to go—although my heart wanted to stay there forever.

It was years later that Kris shared the rest of this story with me. When I left his house that day, his mother looked him in the eyes and proclaimed, "Now, that's the marrying kind!"

Kris protested, "Mom, she's only twelve years old!"

"I don't care if she's ten, that's the kind of woman you should marry," his mom insisted.

Kris told me he realized years later that at the moment of his mother's declaration that day, his heart became open to the possibility of loving me as his wife.

Happily Ever After . . .

A little over a year later, Kris asked me to marry him. I am sure you are already calculating our ages in your head. Yes, I was thirteen years old and Kris was sixteen. It would be four long years later, on July 19, 1975, that I would finally marry the man of my dreams.

Kris is the single greatest gift the Lord has ever given me. There has not been one time in my entire life that I have ever second-guessed my decision to become his bride. When I recited my vows to Kris on that wonderful day in July, I meant every single word: "In good times and in bad . . . in sickness and in health . . . for richer and poor, until death do us part."

Kris has some advice he often gives to people who are on the journey to finding their soul mate and living happily ever after. He tells them, "Don't marry the person you fall in love with. A fall is an accident, not an act of your will. If you fell once, chances are you will fall again for someone else. Instead, grow in love, because what you did on accident you will need to do on purpose. A great marriage is never an accident; it's a covenantal choice that two people make with each other for life. It's only in the soil of sacrifice that the garden of true love can take root in the hearts of its companions."

I have to say that Kris and I have had very different experiences in love. I loved Kris the moment I laid eyes on him, and I knew beyond a shadow of a doubt that he was the one and that I wanted to spend the rest of my life with him. Kris, on the other hand, really liked me when we met and enjoyed my company because he didn't feel as if he had to perform for my love. But it was really "like at first sight" for him, and then he grew to love me over time, as he slowly realized I was the woman he was dreaming of.

> **The truth is that love is not a choice you make once in your life, but a thousand choices you make every day.**

Yet the truth is that love is not a choice you make once in your life, but a thousand choices you make every day. Kris is right about falling in love, because just about the time that the butterflies leave, the cockroaches arrive. If our covenants are based on feelings, the cockroaches will find a way to migrate into our moments of misery and destroy our marriages. But the secret of a great marriage is to do what you do when you feel like it—even when you don't.

In other words, if you think about the way you behave toward your spouse when you *are* "feeling the love," and then you act like that even when you *aren't* feeling a thing, it is likely that you will have an amazing marriage. In the world, actions follow feelings. In the Kingdom, feelings follow actions.

The world is full of broken people who walked away from their covenants when their passion paused and they thought their love was gone. Yet love is like a bear, in that both bears and love can hibernate in the winter and awaken later, in a new season. When the feeling is gone, love hasn't left; it is simply asleep. It can often be awakened by a simple act of kindness. Love never fails.

TWO

IT TAKES A VILLAGE

Let us not lose heart in doing good, for in due time we will reap if we do not grow weary. So then, while we have opportunity, let us do good to all people, and especially to those who are of the household of the faith.

GALATIANS 6:9-10

B end and stretch, reach for the stars, there goes Jupiter, here comes Mars." This was the song that Miss Nancy sang on *Romper Room* (Claster Television, Inc.), a children's TV show I watched as a child in the 1960s, to encourage children to be flexible and pliable. Little did I know that this would become the theme song of my entire life. Only this time, I wouldn't be "playing house" like a child, but I would have the real responsibility of caring for a family of six while passing through the treacherous gauntlet called life.

Kris and I grew up in the San Francisco Bay Area, where they put up a parking lot after they paved paradise, as Joni Mitchell's song "Big

Yellow Taxi" would have put it. Our lives were marked by heavy traffic and hurried commuters wasting their lives on the hamster wheel of self-promotion. Kris was really struggling with anxiety and wanted desperately to exit the hamster cage, but we were not sure how to get through the maze. We worked together at an automotive repair shop, and coincidentally, our boss, Bill Mann, happened to mention that he was taking a fishing trip to a little town called Lewiston that was located in the Trinity Alps of Northern California.

"Would you mind if Kathy and I joined you and your family?" Kris asked.

Bill replied that of course we could come, and that we'd have a blast together. He also mentioned that he knew a great fishing hole, and that the change of pace would do us good.

The trip was exactly what we needed. The serenity of our surroundings quieted our spirits and gave us both a new perspective on life. It was then that we realized something needed to change . . . something radical. When we returned home to the rat race, our hearts yearned for the Shangri-la of the Trinity Alps. For weeks, the trip was all Kris and I could talk about. Back when we were dating, we had dreamed of moving to the country and raising our family there.

One day Kris came home from work with that look in his eye. "How would you like to sell our house and move to Lewiston?" he blurted out.

"You're crazy!" I remarked.

"I'm dead serious, babe," Kris exclaimed. "I'm ready for a change, and I don't want to live under this pressure. I just can't do this anymore," he explained.

By this time, Kris was in the beginning of a nervous breakdown that, unbeknownst to us, would last more than three years. So I knew he was desperate. I wanted the same thing he did, but I was hoping for a long-term plan and a well-thought-out strategy. This scenario gives you a perfect window into our relationship. Kris is a "ready, fire, aim" kind of person, or more accurately, a "jump off the cliff with me, and the water will be there before we hit the ground" kind. So I have spent a good many years hanging on to his hand for dear life.

We went in to work the next morning and explained to Bill what we were feeling. I was prepared for some pushback from him, so I was shocked by his reply. He said he thought it was a great idea, and that he had been thinking of doing the same thing himself since the stress of city life was killing him.

"We'll need to find a place to live," I told Kris. The population of Lewiston was only nine hundred, and I found myself concerned that there might not be many housing options.

> Kris is a "ready, fire, aim" kind of person, or more accurately, a "jump off the cliff with me, and the water will be there before we hit the ground" kind.

"I'll go back to Lewiston and take a look at some different properties, just to get a feel of what's available," Kris suggested. I was unable to go along, so he decided to ask Bill to join him and off they went.

A few days into his trip, Kris called to tell me about a house he had found. "It's perfect for us, babe! It's just like your *Little House on the Prairie* dream. There's a meadow in front of the house, and the property backs up against a mountainside. There's plenty of room for some animals and maybe even a horse! In fact, there's a barn already on the property." Before I could comment, Kris said, "I want you to know that I put in an offer on the house, and it was accepted! Can you believe it?"

I was conflicted—overjoyed on one hand and nervous on the other. Kris picking out our home by himself? This was years before cell phones or even fax machines, so the only thing I had to go on was his commentary on how wonderful the house was.

We put our house up for sale, and we had three offers within 24 hours. We never imagined it was going to sell so quickly. We had so

31

many things to take care of that I was wondering if we could get it all done in time. It was not as if we had tons of furniture, but I was close to my parents and my sister, Rhonda. Reality was slowly setting in, and I was beginning to feel as though this was going to be more difficult than I thought. Not Kris! He had already jumped off the cliff and was eager to put some distance between us and our high-stress life.

Let the Journey Begin

It was the morning of our move, we had finished packing the U-Haul truck, and the last detail we needed to take care of was to deliver our cat that had just had six kittens to my friend's house. Things were moving along uneventfully, until mama cat decided to break out the rear window of our camper shell and leap onto the freeway. Kris immediately pulled over on the side of the road, and we called and called, searching for her. We had seen her run toward a grassy meadow on the other side of a barbed-wire fence, so thankfully we knew she was alive. But she didn't come back; she was gone from me forever!

> This trip was going to be a memory maker for sure! Plus, our five-hour drive had just gotten a lot longer.

I could not believe it. This was not how I thought our trip was going to start. *Now what am I going to do?* I thought to myself. *My cat that I love is gone, and we're left with six two-day-old kittens without a mother!*

The only right thing to do was bundle up the kittens warmly and try to feed them with an eyedropper every two hours. This trip was going to be a memory maker for sure! Plus, our five-hour drive had just gotten a lot longer with the added stops to take care of the kittens. Did I mention that we also had a German shepherd, an Irish Setter and a four-month-old baby with us? Yikes!

We finally arrived at our new house at 4:30 a.m. It was a moonless night, which meant it was pitch black in the mountains. You couldn't see your hand in front of your face. We made our way to the back door with a small flashlight, only to discover that Kris had forgotten to have the electricity turned on. Consequently, we had no running water either, because the house had a well that required electricity to pump water to the house.

To make matters worse, it was literally freezing inside the house. But we were all so exhausted that the only thing we wanted to do was sleep. We rolled out our sleeping bags, laid them on the floor and crashed. Our daughter Jaime was a trooper. She was totally oblivious to our new adventure and was perfectly happy to sleep in her portable bassinet.

The Dawn of a New Era

I woke early the next morning and thought, *Where the heck am I?* Bright light was streaming in through the window, shining on my face. My body ached everywhere, and something smelled really, really bad. The odor was coming up from the ancient and dirty carpet we were lying on. I rolled over to see if Kris was awake, only to spy spiders crawling on his sleeping bag. I jumped up quickly and was greeted by his smiling face, along with a hungry baby.

"Good morning, honey!" Kris proclaimed. "I had the electricity turned on already. Welcome to our new home."

I have to admit, the surroundings were beautiful. The house, however, was trashed. First things first—we commenced a mad hunt for the thermostat and cranked that baby up to 70 degrees. It was 35 degrees inside, so cold, in fact, that you could see your breath. Jaime's little lips were blue. We quickly grabbed our jackets and made our way through our new living quarters. It was a typical old farmhouse. There were three bedrooms plastered with old, musty wallpaper—half of it shredded and falling off the walls.

We walked down the hall to the kitchen. The old cupboards had needed an upgrade about forty years earlier. The white paint was dingy and needed a good scrubbing. Attached to the kitchen was a mud room with a single toilet off to the side. Every farmhouse needs a good mud room, and this one had it all, including the mud.

> **Every farmhouse needs a good mud room, and this one had it all, including the mud.**

"I can't wait to show you the property," Kris said. "The house even has a front deck." (Although we soon discovered that the entire deck was rotted out.)

I slid open the heavy sliding glass window and stepped outside. I was so excited to be able to see our dream finally coming to pass.

"Look!" Kris said. "There's even a barn and a corral."

Now this is what I'm talking about, I thought to myself. I hurried over to the barn, threw back the door and walked inside.

"Wow," I said. The stalls looked as if there had been pigs living in them. The boards on the walls were rotten, there were huge holes in the roof and the barn stunk so bad from wet, rotten manure that I thought I was going to puke. I heard a clacking noise on the ground, and all of a sudden about a dozen chickens and one mad rooster came running toward us.

"So we have chickens now?" I asked.

"The previous owners said they were going to leave a few things for us, but I had no idea they meant chickens," Kris confessed.

We left the barn and began walking the property. We made our way to the front yard, which was a beautiful meadow of flowers, but was also filled with old cars and trash.

"Are the previous owners going to clean this up?" I inquired with a frown.

"I knew there was some junk that needed to be taken to the dump, but the owners said they had already cleaned it up," Kris replied, looking bewildered.

This is crazy, I thought. *We probably have about three months of cleanup to do.* I have to admit, I was pretty discouraged.

The next day, Kris and I decided we would tackle the projects one at a time. The first order of business was to remove the carpet from the house. We worked together, pulling up the edges and trying to roll the carpet up in sections.

"I can't believe this!" I said. The carpet would not roll up; it just broke into little pieces, as if it were petrified. We decided we would have to shovel it out by hand. It took hours and hours to remove it all. The house had been built in the early sixties, and I don't think the previous owners had ever replaced the carpet in all the years they had lived there.

Along with the fossilized carpet, our shovels were filled with dead, gross spiders, bugs, dirt and animal hair. It creeped me out to think that just the night before, we were sleeping on top of all that. *I'm living the dream now,* I thought to myself, *but it's more like a nightmare!*

Kris felt really bad. "I never should have bought this house without you seeing it first," he said with a sad look on his face.

"Don't worry, honey," I said, teasing him. "We said *for better or for worse.*" We both laughed. "It's all good," I continued, yet two hours later it was still freezing inside the house. "We need to get the propane tank filled up. I'll call the gas company in the morning."

Just then, a man came knocking on our back door. He was a rugged-looking mountain man about six-foot-five, lean but strong, with long, frizzy hair pulled back into a ponytail. His jeans and shirt had obviously seen some hard workdays.

"Hey there!" he said in a raspy voice. "I'm your neighbor across the way. Name's Paul. I noticed there's no smoke coming out of your chimney. Aren't you guys building a fire? You must be freezing!"

"Something must be wrong with the thermostat on the wall, because we can't get the furnace to work," Kris explained.

"Thermostat? That thermostat hasn't worked in over twenty years!" He chuckled.

"I'm sure the tank is just out of propane," Kris said.

"Think what you want there, but that propane tank hasn't ever been hooked up to anything. The only thing that'll warm this place up is the woodstove."

"Where do we buy wood?" Kris inquired.

Paul chuckled at that question and said we wouldn't be buying wood anywhere around there; we'd need to cut it down ourselves. He offered to take Kris out to cut some right then and there, since he didn't want his new neighbors freezing to death.

Kris didn't have any boots, but a few minutes later he jumped into Paul's old truck and headed for the backwoods. Kris and Paul returned at dusk, both covered in wood chips. Kris's face was black with dirt, and his teeth looked as if he had been chewing tobacco. He moved like an eighty-year-old man. I have never seen my man so stinking exhausted. He struggled to stack the wood they had cut and split as Paul chucked it to him from the bed of the truck, taunting him as they worked: "Come on, boy, get the lead out! Keep it going; there's more where that came from!"

> In the mountains, your neighbors become your friends and your friends become your family.

I can't tell you how much I appreciated raising our family in a small mountain community. There is nothing like it. When you live in the mountains, far from society, you have to depend on your neighbors just to get through everyday life. You forge a strong bond with them because you are struggling together to survive the often-treacherous conditions of wilderness living. Nobody gives a rip about the political or religious affiliations of their neighbors, because real friendship transcends people's opinions.

In the mountains, your neighbors become your friends and your friends become your family. I will never forget the kindness of our neighbors, who always had time to come to our rescue. Our new community was a place where the saying "it takes a village to raise a child" certainly applied. I do know for sure that it took a mountain community to raise the Vallotton clan. It was there that we learned the true meaning of "family."

We all need a Paul in our life—a person who is not afraid to speak the truth or hurt our feelings. It was imperative that we had someone to learn from in our new lifestyle. Paul and his wife, Lorna, were not blood relatives, but they were "family" in every sense of the word. Kris and I would not have made it through our first year in the mountains without their input into our lives.

The Other Villagers

There would be many more "Pauls" and "Lornas" who would emerge in our lives throughout the twenty years that we lived in the Trinity Alps. We lived out our mountain journey in four different homes during those two decades, and every time we moved, it felt as though God divinely arranged our neighbors.

For example, years later, when we were living in Weaverville, which was about fifteen miles from Lewiston, our daughters, Jaime and Shannon, were in their early teens. They began spending a lot of time at our neighbors' house across the way. When I asked them what they were doing at Jeff and Jackie's house so much, their response was, "We're just hanging out." As they got older, the girls seemed to spend more and more time over there, and I started to feel really jealous. I remember thinking that I was losing my girls to the woman next door—someone younger, prettier and probably wiser than I was. My girls and I had always been close; we did everything together. Yet when Jackie stepped into the picture, I felt as if my "alone time" with my girls was being challenged.

It was a really difficult season for me. One day, I couldn't take it any longer. I finally broke down in tears and talked to Kris about how I was processing this new season of our girls' lives. I remember him telling me, "You can't be everything to our kids. It's really good for the girls to have a relationship with other healthy women. That doesn't mean that the kids love you less. They just need someone else besides you that they can confide in. Someone who makes them feel safe."

I remembered other people's kids who had confided in me the same way my girls were trusting Jackie. I wondered if their parents had resented me for having that place in their kids' lives. *I sure hope not*, I mused. It would never be my intention to take the place of another child's parent, just as it was never Jackie's intention to try to take mine. Yet it often is just easier for our kids to hear what we have been trying to tell them from someone else.

Villagers Unite

No matter whether you live in a mountain community or a massive city, we all need neighbors to help us through life. I am reminded of Mary and Joseph, who apparently lost Jesus for three days. Candidly, I don't know how you misplace the Son of God for three days, but that's what happened. Of course, Jesus ended up being in the Temple, dialoguing with the religious leaders, which means technically He wasn't really lost. He hadn't run away or anything like that, thankfully. But the part of the story that has always intrigued me is that His parents didn't even know He was missing for a while, because it was so common for children to spend time with other families in those days. I suppose this shows that it has always taken a village!

It seems to me that the challenges of raising children today are so much greater than they were in any other generation in recent history. With nearly 50 percent of all the babies in America born out of wedlock, fatherlessness has become a pandemic. Then add to this mess the rising divorce rate, and we can see the need of having a "healthy village" around us to raise children. It has become essential. If raising children in a healthy family, with both parents present and accounted for, is tough in today's sin-filled world, then single parents must be some kind of multitasking miracle workers.

We experienced this firsthand when our son Jason went through his divorce. Jason had his three kids nearly full time for the first few years. It was grueling for him, realizing that he could not give his kids everything they needed. Yet Jason had a healthy team of villagers around him and his family. They stepped in and helped him steady the boat, so to speak. He had spent years helping out the "villagers" in his life, and when they realized he and his children were in trouble, they lined up at his door to help him fill the family gap. Oftentimes, he would come home to a stocked refrigerator, clean clothes and dinner on the table. It was pretty humbling, but he needed the help and it was his turn to be the receiver instead of the giver. His children bonded to the villagers in those days, and those people became their lifeline.

God knows how to take a mess and make it a miracle.

Nobody goes into a relationship thinking, *I hope this ends terribly.* We all go in looking forward to a bright future together. We have plans and dreams for our families, and we want to see them fulfilled. But things happen. Life happens, and people make bad choices that we have no control over. If you find yourself in a situation like Jason's and you think your life is over, let me tell you, it's not! God knows how to take a mess and make it a miracle.

I want to encourage you to find your "village people" and serve them like your own family. You just never know when you will need them. And when you do need them, humble yourself and let them know. Nobody should ever have to suffer alone or suffer in silence. I am convinced that God looks ahead at our challenges and troubles and divinely moves the right people into our neighborhood at the perfect time, or He moves us into the right neighborhood. Our children don't have to live a fatherless or motherless existence if we live among healthy villagers.

I would like to suggest that if you are in a tough situation, the first thing you need to do is find a healthy village. Even if you are looking for another spouse to add to your life and your children's, it is good to know that healthy villagers make better parents and better spouses!

THREE

THE REST OF THE STORY

Love empowers us to fulfill the law of the Anointed
One as we carry each other's troubles.

GALATIANS 6:2 TPT

I told you about Kris's anxiety, which helped propel us toward leaving the Bay Area and moving to the Trinity Alps to find a slower way of life. The fact is, there's a ton more to the story. Kris wrote a book about this trying season in his life, *Spirit Wars*, which often inspires his readers and listeners to ask me how I helped him through his dark night of the soul. As I fill in a few more details about the situation leading up to his emotional crash and everything that followed, you will see how I processed through it myself and how I was able to support him through it.

41

Kris was extremely busy at the auto repair shop. Bill Mann had promoted him to shop foreman when Kris was nineteen, and Kris had eleven men working for him, most of whom were a lot older than he was. Let's just say the situation put Kris in the position of "learning how to manage people." The absence of leadership training in his life, added to a fatherless upbringing, certainly had not prepared him for managing others. He resorted to driving his men like a drill sergeant preparing cadets for war.

This approach was all validated and justified in Kris's mind by his upbringing, because his grandfather had taught him the value of hard work, long hours and taking pride in the outcome. To this day, his work ethic is impeccable. He can run circles around most people, even people much younger than he is. He expected his repair shop team to follow his example, which was good. Yet when they couldn't perform at his level, it became a major problem. Consequently, the shop was experiencing record profits under Kris's leadership, which made his boss happy, but it was putting a huge amount of stress on Kris's relationships with his men.

> **Many nights I found myself crying myself to sleep, feeling as though I was a failure as a wife—especially since the littlest job around the house became a monster glaring in my face.**

Furthermore, customers loved the quality of the shop's work, so it became busier and busier. This led to Kris working twelve-hour shifts most days, and coming home completely exhausted. This pattern continued after we were married and I became the shop's bookkeeper. We had been married for less than a year when I discovered I was pregnant. Determined to keep up my "normal pace" (more like a normal "Kris pace"), I would drag myself into work until the nausea would overtake my body and I would have to go home. The situation continued day after day, until I finally gave in and called it quits.

I was not used to being incapacitated. It was difficult being relegated to a couch all day, unable to move due to an unwelcome upheaval every twenty minutes. Many nights I found myself crying myself to sleep, feeling as though I was a failure as a wife—especially since the littlest job around the house became a monster glaring in my face. It took everything I had within me to get through a "normal" day. Every day was a challenge for me, yet the biggest challenge for us had not even reared its ugly little head yet. . . .

The On-Ramp to Oppression

Then came that fateful night when I was lying on the couch and all of a sudden heard Kris yell out for me to come into the bathroom. I was about seven months pregnant at the time, and I was not moving very quickly.

"Something's wrong with me!" Kris shouted. "I can't stop shaking! I think I'm having a heart attack!"

I grabbed a towel and helped Kris get out of the bathtub. My mind was freaking out. *What's happening with my husband?* I thought. I tried everything I could think of to get him to calm down. Nothing worked! I decided to call our doctor to see if he could help. I finally got him on the phone, and he asked me several questions.

"Kris isn't having a heart attack," our doctor proceeded to tell me after I had answered his questions. "He's having a panic attack. He's under too much stress. His lifestyle needs to change at work so that his body has time to rest," our good doctor advised.

Our doctor was also one of our best customers at the auto repair shop, so he understood the culture of Kris's workplace. But unbeknownst to the doctor, Kris was also living on candy bars and soda pop. As the weeks went on after the bathtub incident, Kris did not improve at all, although he was somewhat better at work because his mind was so busy there. At least the distractions made his anxiety bearable. But as soon as he got home, he became a different person.

I tried my best to help Kris walk through this nightmare, but initially I didn't have any success. Part of it was that I was fighting my own battle with a tough pregnancy, and I felt quite guilty about it because I was the one who had wanted a baby. Kris had wanted to wait a few years. I reasoned that Kris was working much too hard because of the new addition to our family, and it was all my fault. (Looking back now, I can see that this was Kris's issue, and it was not my fault.)

Many of Kris's friends tried to reach out to help him, but Kris was not interested in being around anyone but me. He would hear a knock at the door and run into the master bedroom, where he would lock himself in and beg me to get rid of whoever was at the door. At night, he would have such intense night sweats that I would have to get up and change the sheets. We would try to go to church on Sundays, but that was a huge ordeal. If Kris was not sitting in an aisle seat next to a door, he couldn't stay in the building without having anxiety attacks. These scenarios repeated themselves over and over again for three long years.

Bonding or Breaking

Walking through hard times with someone you love will either bond you or break you, especially relationally. Trials don't cause your problems; trials reveal them. I was determined to love the "hell" out of Kris and let the fiery furnace of the hardest trial of his life weld us together at the very core of our beings. I could see the pain and fear that lived in his eyes, and the question that kept going through his mind: *Is this hell ever going to end?*

Kris was in such turmoil that there was no way I was going to allow the stuff I was going through to spill out onto him. I was a mature woman and could lean on God to help me handle my intense morning sickness. Besides, there was nothing that Kris could do to make me feel better.

A funny side note is that when Kris and I were first married, we were talking one night, and he suddenly grabbed my hand and held it tightly in his. With a dead-serious look in his eyes, he stared straight into mine and said, "If one of us is ever down, the other one needs to be up. . . . Promise me that we will never both be down at the same time!"

Trials don't cause your problems; trials reveal them.

I think he was halfway joking, but our promise to one another to support each other through life's lows became one of our goals in hard times. Thankfully, we have not had to face that situation very often. When it has happened, however, we do our very best not to stay there. We don't always get to choose what runs through our minds, but we do have a choice about what kind of thoughts move in and rent a room there.

Let There Be Life

The time finally came for me to give birth to our first child. I was three weeks past due, so my labor was supposed to be induced on a Monday morning. The previous Sunday night, I went into labor on my own. Kris was trying to be strong for me, although he obviously had his own issues going on. But we finally got to the hospital and got settled into my room.

Kris and I had taken a Lamaze natural childbirth class together because I thought it would be a great way for us to connect during the delivery. (Kris hated it!) The basic principles of the class (according to Kris) were that he was supposed to create a focal point that I could concentrate on during my labor pains, to take my mind off the intense discomfort. Then he was supposed to get close to my face and help coach my breathing, to ease the pain during contractions. But that plan didn't actually go so well for us. The story goes something like this: Kris put a Snickers bar on a shelf in front of me, to act as my focal point. About twelve hours into my labor, I was yelling at him, which made him so nervous that he ate the focal point! (Someday you have to hear him tell the story.)

> **Kris put a Snickers bar on a shelf in front of me, to act as my focal point. About twelve hours into my labor ... he ate the focal point!**

The truth is that something didn't feel quite right during my labor. At one point, suddenly doctors and interns started coming in and out of my room in groups of two or three. After examining me, they would congregate outside my door, where I could hear their muffled words as they conversed back and forth. By now I had been in labor for eighteen hours. I was exhausted, and I was worried about how Kris was holding up (especially since he thought I was yelling at him). Soon my doctor came back in and informed us that the baby had moved transverse inside me.

"What does that mean?" I asked.

"Your baby's head is no longer engaged in the birth canal, and its body has turned sideways in your womb," the doctor said. "I'm going to take you into the delivery room right now."

We were in the delivery room for ten more hours. Kris kept passing out in the room from stress, and he required assistance from the doctor. Every few hours, the doctor would give Kris smelling salts because he kept passing out on the floor. When the baby finally came out, the doctor turned to Kris and asked, "Do you want to cut the umbilical cord?"

Kris snapped back, "No! What the heck do we pay you guys to do?"

A few seconds later, the doctor cut the cord, and the nurse tried to hand our baby girl to Kris. Jaime was covered in blood, of course, which must have taken him by surprise.

Kris looked at the nurse and said, "I waited nine months for this little girl. I can wait five more minutes for you to clean her up!"

Everyone cracked up, which lightened the mood. But between Kris and me, I don't know who was more exhausted.

Certainty in Uncertain Times

The pain of childbirth was intense for me, but beyond that, watching Kris go through a nervous breakdown was one of the hardest things I have ever had to walk through personally. I think the toughest part of the entire ordeal was the uncertainty of not knowing if he was ever going to be back to "normal" again. My emotions seemed tethered to his condition. On his really dark days, I would often catch myself drowning in despair, searching for some kind of life preserver of hope.

Part of my challenge was that Kris has always been the confident one in our relationship. I was accustomed to being his encourager, but not his supporter, his defender and his counselor. I had to find a way to untie myself from Kris's condition and tie myself to something stable . . . not just for me, but for both of us.

I soon realized that although our situation was unstable, God's love for us was not. His plan for our lives is not determined by our strength, but by His. In fact, God convinced me that when we are weak, He is strong, and that actually, His strength is perfected in our weakness. I began to see Kris's weakness, his frailty and his humble state as a tremendous advantage in Jesus. I could see that he was walking through the valley of the shadow of death, but where there is a shadow, there has to be, by necessity, a light.

I came to understand that this was Kris's caterpillar season. Something powerful and profound was happening in his darkness, and at

> I soon realized that although our situation was unstable, God's love for us was not.

47

the right time, in the proper season, God's beauty and power would be exposed to a hurting and broken world. God was molding His man in obscurity to impact a world in disparity, and to bring prisoners out of captivity, into a place of wholeness and serenity. My only job was to believe God!

FOUR

BUSINESS UNUSUAL

Within your heart you can make plans for your future,
but the Lord chooses the steps you take to get there.

PROVERBS 16:9 TPT

I loved our Lewiston home. I was so happy there, and my life felt complete. We had two little kids, two dogs and six ducks that Kris had brought home for the kids for Easter one year. Needless to say, I was busy. I was born to be a mom, and I loved every part of it. Of course, there were challenges. There always are. But I was ready to take on whatever came my way.

Kris finally began to recover from his nervous breakdown, and although he was not completely well, life was slowly returning to normal. We started having friends over again, which Kris had put on hold for three years while he recovered. One evening, Kris told me he was bringing a guy over whom he had met at church. He said the guy was a prophet and had a prophetic word for Kris.

Now, let me be clear—the whole prophet thing was still all very new to us. We had met a couple of prophets who came to our little church in Weaverville once a year, but we had never had a one-on-one sit-down with them. I have to admit that I felt a bit intimidated.

The night arrived and a man named Patrick came over to our house. I fixed dinner, the guys talked and the kids were . . . well, being kids. Most of the evening was filled with small talk and swapping Scripture references back and forth that were dear to our hearts. By the time we sat down for dinner, Patrick was telling us stories of miracles he had seen. This guy was really interesting and a little scary, yet I was beginning to feel more and more comfortable as the evening went on. Then Patrick abruptly ended his story and began to tell Kris what he felt the Lord was showing him.

"I feel as though the Lord is opening up a business opportunity for you," Patrick prophesied. "God says if you will open a business, He will bless you!"

I looked over at Kris, who was squirming in his seat. I could tell that he was really bothered by this word. He heard Patrick out and then told him, "I don't want to go into business. I want to be a pastor!"

I knew this was coming because Kris had received four other prophecies that same week about going into business. A couple of days earlier, on Sunday afternoon, our leadership team had been having lunch with Dick Mills, a traveling minister. He had suddenly interrupted our lunch to give Kris a prophetic word: "God is going to give you double wisdom for business—the wisdom of man and the wisdom of God."

> "God is going to give you double wisdom for business—the wisdom of man and the wisdom of God."

Kris left the restaurant mad. When we got in the car, he proclaimed, "I don't want to be in business! I want to be in the ministry!" To make matters worse, our good friend Charlie Harper had taken Kris to work the Monday morning after Dick's word. That morning, Charlie had told Kris that he had a dream about him owning the Union 76 station in town. You can imagine how that went over! After all that, Kris was not ready to hear it again from Patrick.

"Hey, brother," Patrick said afterward, "I'm just telling you what I heard the Lord tell me. If you don't like the word, go take it up with Him."

Soon Patrick left, and I was cleaning up the kitchen when Kris walked in. He was so frustrated. "I don't want to go into business," he insisted. "Patrick is wrong!"

I wasn't going to argue with Kris; I knew it wouldn't do much good anyway. His mind was made up. In fact, for the last few years Kris had been doing everything that he could to serve our pastor, Bill Johnson. Moreover, Kris loved reading his Bible, and God was giving him real insight. He just needed an opportunity to do ministry, and it was not going to happen being in business. Or so he thought.

Grandma Gets Us Going

Friday rolled around, and Kris came home from work with an announcement: "You'll never believe who called me today. The owner of the Union 76 station in town," he proclaimed.

"I don't think I've ever met him," I remarked. "What was he calling you for?"

"You'll never believe this!" Kris continued. "He wants to sell the 76 station, and he wants me to buy it!"

I felt a tickle of excitement that went through my body. "And . . . ?"

"I told him I wasn't interested."

"Just like that?" I asked. "Aren't you even going to pray about it?"

"Oh, I did. . . . He wants a lot of money down, and we don't have any money. It's plain and simple, don't you think?" Kris questioned.

"You've always told me that we shouldn't let money stop us from doing anything, and that God will come through if it's His will and His timing," I said. "I think you need to call Grandma and talk to her about it. Maybe she'll lend you the money."

> Kris can be tough on the outside, but I always know how to get to him.

"Are you kidding me?" he declared. "She wouldn't lend her own son money when he was in trouble. What makes you think that she'll lend me money?"

"I don't know," I said. "I just think that you should try."

Kris can be tough on the outside, but I always know how to get to him. A few hours later, Kris was on the phone with his grandma. After hemming and hawing around for a bit, he finally got up enough nerve to tell her about this new opportunity that had been offered to him. He presented her with all the details, and finally, after about fifteen minutes, he hung up the phone.

"So, what did she say?" I asked. "*What did she say?*" I asked louder.

"I can't believe it! She said she wouldn't loan me the money."

"I am so sorry!" I said.

Kris turned, looked me in the eyes and said, "She's *giving* me the money! Nine thousand dollars, to be exact."

I could not believe my ears. I had encouraged him to ask his grandmother for the loan, but never did I imagine that she would just give it to him. It seemed as if God's perfect will for us was being laid out right before our eyes. It caused Kris to second-guess his "I want to be in the ministry" mindset. It was a great day for a celebration!

"Too God" of an Opportunity

We knew that buying a business of our own would mean a huge shift in our family life, although we had no idea what that was going to look like. I am one who does not like change, but in this unique moment it seemed like too good—or should I say "too God"—an opportunity to pass up.

Kris called the owner of the 76 station while I listened in. He asked if he could meet him sometime the next week. There was some small talk back and forth, and then I heard Kris say, "Great! I'll see you then."

The day arrived, and Kris sheepishly left the house for his meeting. I can remember asking God, *If this business deal is supposed to happen, set everything up so we can't fail, and please help us have all the money we need to close the deal.*

Now, that was a big "ask," but I knew that our God could do miracles. A long time passed, and I was growing impatient waiting for Kris to get home. Five hours later, he finally walked through the door. We sat down, and Kris shared the whole story with me. I don't think he left out any of the details, either, because I was drilling him like a sergeant drills a private. He told me that they had come to an agreement on the price of the station, and that they both thought it would be best if Kris quit his job at the tire shop and managed the station until the escrow closed. (He actually ended up getting fired when his boss found out he was leaving.)

"Wow," I said. "That's pretty amazing that the owner would do that for us." Our future was looking brighter and brighter.

We opened a thirty-day escrow at the title company for the sale of the business. When we were within a few days of closing the deal, which required the $9,000 down payment, the escrow company started calling and asking us to bring our check to the title company. Kris let the caller know that the money would be there in plenty of time and thanked him for the reminder. What Kris did not tell him was that we were $1,400 short of meeting our escrow obligation.

What are we going to do now? I wondered.

The truth is, we had been running the station for a month under the previous owner's name, and everything was going great—until it wasn't. In the first two weeks of operating the business, one of our staff forgot to park a U.S. Forest Service truck inside the shop at night.

The truth is, we had been running the station for a month under the previous owner's name, and everything was going great—until it wasn't.

It had four brand-new tires and rims in the back of the bed. When we arrived at work the next morning, the tires and rims were gone. They had been stolen, and Kris felt sick about it. We didn't have insurance yet, so to cover the cost of a new set of wheels and tires, we had to use some of the escrow money his grandmother had given us.

Honestly, that first month at the station was becoming a disaster as several other unplanned expenses kept rearing their ugly heads. Things were not looking good.

A couple of days later, Kris received another call. "Escrow closes in one more day," the escrow company man warned. "You have to have your money in by tomorrow morning."

"Okay," Kris replied. "I got it handled."

Kris called to let me know that we only had one day left to get all the money together and get it to the title company. "I don't know where we're going to get the rest of the down payment," he confessed. "This was a bad idea! We never should have gone through with this purchase," he muttered.

A little later in the day, Kris was lying on a creeper, working underneath a truck, when a customer came up to him and handed him some money. He recognized the guy's voice and knew it was a good friend of his. He assumed that the man was paying for his self-serve gas, so he thanked him and put the money in his shirt pocket.

His friend said, "Kris, you might want to take a look at that money I just gave you."

Puzzled, Kris rolled out from underneath the truck and pulled the money out of his pocket. It was fourteen brand-new $100 bills!

"Where did you get all that money?" Kris inquired.

"It's not from me. A guy asked me to give it to you," his friend replied.

Kris was in tears at that point, and a few moments later he called me on the phone. "You are never going to believe what just happened!"

I can't tell you how many times I have heard the phrase from Kris, "You are never going to believe what just happened!" This time when he said it, I was not sure whether to brace myself for life to punch me in the face or put on my dancing shoes. The suspense caused me to reflect quickly on our situation and remind myself of God's faithfulness. I knew that every opportunity, good or bad, was an invitation for God to do what only He can do in our lives. But my personal dilemma was that we were so short on the down payment, and so many things were going wrong in our new business, that I was having a hard time reconciling God's prophetic promise to us with our current reality.

> **I can't tell you how many times I have heard the phrase from Kris, "You are never going to believe what just happened!"**

"Kris, I hate suspense! Just give me the news," I scolded. A moment later, however, I was dancing a jig and praising God right there in our kitchen!

The escrow closed the next day, and we sailed away from the safe harbor of predictability into the treacherous waters of risk and reward. Little did we know at the time that when God had said He would "bless us if we opened a business," His idea of blessing and our idea of blessing were not the same.

FIVE

TROUBLE IN PARADISE

Trust in the Lord completely, and do not rely on your own opinions. With all your heart rely on him to guide you, and he will lead you in every decision you make. Become intimate with him in whatever you do, and he will lead you wherever you go.

PROVERBS 3:5–6 TPT

In the midst of the unfolding prophecy of our Union 76 station, while we were learning how to navigate the challenges of everyday "Holy Spirit entrepreneurship," someone asked me, "What do you dream about, Kathy?"

I sat there rummaging around in my brain, trying to think of one dream that I could share with her. A few minutes passed, and I finally looked up at her and said, "I can't think of one thing!"

When I was dating Kris, I had so many dreams. I dreamed of being a wife and a mom, and of living out in the country somewhere where we could have lots of land. I can remember daydreaming for hours about what it would be like to move to a place like Walnut Grove, the setting for the long-running show *Little House on the Prairie*. That was my favorite show. I would make up stories in my mind of living on the Ingalls homestead and loving life, just as Laura Ingalls had done so many years ago. Kris thinks I was born one hundred years too late. Hard work, country life and a boatload of animals suit me just fine. Who needs cars when you can jump on the back of a horse and ride off into the sunset?

> Kris thinks I was born one hundred years too late. Hard work, country life and a boatload of animals suit me just fine.

Our old farmhouse days in Lewiston were short-lived, however. I loved the property and the fact that it felt as if we were living in the middle of nowhere. But Kris didn't share that same opinion. Since he was working in Weaverville, he wanted to move closer into town, where his commute would be shorter and our friends would be closer.

"I guarantee you we will buy some land and build our dream house!" Kris said. "You won't regret selling the farmhouse, I promise." So we put my "little house on the prairie" (which we had fixed up) on the market, and it soon sold.

The Big Move

Closing day arrived, and we packed up the old farmhouse and moved everything to a rental house. Saying "good-bye" to our little place was so sad, even though it was not as if we would never see it again. We often found ourselves driving by just to take a look at what the new owners were doing to it. I kept telling myself, *We're leaving the past and looking to the future!* Besides, Kris had said that our next house would be everything we dreamed of. I couldn't wait to see what the future had in store for us.

We purchased a one-acre parcel of land in the woods and began building the home of our dreams. We were beyond excited! I can't tell you the number of nights that we stayed up late, planning each room of our house. There were so many times when I would pinch myself just to make sure I was not asleep, fearing that I would wake up and none of it would be true. But the dream was happening, and it was real.

Building a house was much harder than I thought it would be. You have only one chance to do it right, and we didn't want to mess up. Some months into the construction of our new home, however, we discovered that our contractor had messed up the timeline for its completion and it would be several more months before we could move in. We had been in our rental house for eight months, while we were building our house. To make matters worse, the owner of the house we were renting called to inform us that he was putting his house on the market, so we would need to move out in the next thirty days. Kris and I already felt enough stress with the construction of our own home being delayed. We did not need to add rental house hunting to our growing list of things to do. We knew it was not going to be easy to find a place to rent for six months, especially one that would allow us to bring our two large dogs, six ducks and now a pet rat with us.

One afternoon, Kris and I shared our dilemma with Bill and Beni Johnson. They both graciously decided to open up their small home for us to move into. I cannot tell you how relieved and excited we were to be able to live with the Johnsons. A couple of weeks later, we put our furniture in storage, found someone to take our ducks, grabbed the dogs and our pet rat and moved in with the Johnsons. Life was . . . well, a little cramped, but so good.

The Johnson house was very small even for one family, let alone two. Our room was about ten by twelve feet, furnished with a double bed and dresser. But Kris and I, along with our kids, ages two and four, had a nice, cozy place to call home for a few months.

I put our rat's cage in the family room, until Beni told me that Bill hated rats. "You're going to have to keep him with you in your room," Beni insisted with a laugh.

"No problem!" I said. There was always room for one more.

We learned so much during those few months of living with the Johnsons. Our kids were very young, and the Johnson kids, Eric and Brian at the time, were just a few months older than our girls, Jaime and Shannon. Eric was always happy and full of energy. Brian was more on the quiet side and loved to snuggle. When the boys would play together, there was a whoosh of energy all around, complete with sound effects and little bodies going everywhere. Their voices were loud and nonstop, which we weren't accustomed to. Shannon could kind of keep up with the boys, but Jaime was so quiet and reserved.

I loved watching Bill and Beni interact with their kids. They were both so wise in areas that we were not. Like the times when Bill would be in an important meeting with leaders, and his boys would be totally oblivious to his conversation, as little ones often are. They would interrupt him, and Bill would graciously excuse himself from his important conversation, saying, "Excuse me a moment while I answer my boys' questions." He would take the time to talk to his kids, and then he would quietly remind them that he was in a meeting and that they could ask more questions later. Those boys always knew they were loved. Bill and Beni never pushed them aside to entertain grown-ups.

> **We were often so busy trying to make a living in our business that sometimes we forgot that first and foremost, we were supposed to be making a difference in our family.**

The Johnsons' kids were celebrated, not tolerated. Personally, I had never seen this kind of child/parent interaction displayed in such a beautiful way before.

Kris and I had so much to learn! Living with Bill and Beni forced me to think about our parenting priorities. We were often so busy trying to make a living in our business that sometimes we forgot that first and foremost, we were supposed to be making a difference in our family. The Johnsons' example reminded me over and over that there was nothing in life as important as our family. In those days, my mind would frequently wander back to our dating years, when I had daydreamed for hours about what it would be like to have a family and what it would be like to teach our kids how to grow up healthy and strong, loving God and the people around them. I made a commitment during those days at the Johnsons' to put God, my husband and my kids first and to keep them there, as the most important thing in my life. I have kept that covenant to this day. Sometimes, we need to renew our minds about the things that once were so important to us, but that somehow got lost in the busyness of life.

It Is Finished

After six months of living with the Johnsons, our house was finally complete. I can't tell you how excited I was to be moving into a place that we had designed ourselves and then contracted to be built just the way we imagined it. I am sure that Bill and Beni were glad to have their space back, especially since we had stayed with them much longer than we had anticipated.

We moved into our dream chalet in the summer of 1979 and lived there until 1997. We raised all our children in that home back in the woods. We made so many memories there, watching our children grow from babies into teenagers, with all the laughter and tears that come with raising a family. We celebrated eighteen white Christmases on that land, and we loved every minute of our journey. We practiced the things we learned from the Johnsons, and those principles shaped our children.

> **The automotive business was tough, especially in the dead of winter.... You could literally shoot a cannonball down Main Street in that weather and not strike a single car.**

While we were living out my "little house on the prairie" dream at home, we were struggling to build our business to support our family. The 76 station was only our first purchase, after which we started several other businesses during the twenty years that we lived in the mountains. Kris and I were great business partners, but growing businesses in the Trinity Alps was no small feat. The automotive business was tough, especially in the dead of winter, with two feet of snow on the ground and freezing temperatures. You could literally shoot a cannonball down Main Street in that weather and not strike a single car.

I oversaw the financial side of our businesses, while Kris managed the daily operations. (I will tell you in the next chapter how I became the bookkeeper.) Our businesses grew every year, and this created a need for more and more cash. By our tenth year in business, along with the Union 76 service station, we also were running a fleet repair shop, an import car repair shop and an auto parts store—all at the same time. I became very creative in learning new ways to stretch a dollar, but even that skill can only go so far. I was under lots of stress at work, and it began wearing on me. I decided to move my office to our house instead of having to go to work at the parts store every day. My new home office was cozy, and things were working out pretty well—until they were not.

The Long Winter

One of my worst memories is the winter of 1989. Three feet of snow was on the ground, and none of our shop customers were paying their auto parts bills. We had about thirty employees who were all depending on their paychecks to feed their families, but we had not taken a paycheck ourselves in a couple of months. To make matters worse, I was getting about forty phone calls a week from our suppliers, all of them asking for money.

At first, it was no big deal. I am great at organization and love strategizing new ways to solve old problems. In fact, I thrive on it. But even I was getting worn out by the stress. I was losing my peace and my refuge. I soon realized that I had made a big mistake moving my office into our home. I could not escape the pressure; it was everywhere!

One late afternoon, Kris called me at home. "Hey, baby, did you pay the warehouse for last month's purchases?"

Taking a moment, I responded, "Yes, I wrote them a check."

"The warehouse manager told me he hasn't received his check yet," Kris said.

"The mail must be a bit slow. He should have it by tomorrow," I responded.

Before hanging up, Kris said he would call the manager back and tell him what I had said. I hung up the phone and began to shake. I was truly losing it! I just sat there staring at the check I hadn't mailed, and all the employee time cards that were in front of me, and prayed, *God, if I've ever needed a miracle, now is the time!* My mind was flooded with terrible thoughts: *You are such a failure, and everybody knows it. You're a loser, a liar and a cheat!*

Early the next morning, the phone rang, and it was Kris on the line again. "Hey, I was spending some time praying this morning and God said you needed to tell me something."

"Really? What's that?" I asked.

"God told me that you weren't telling me the truth yesterday, and that you didn't write a check to the warehouse," he continued in a soft voice.

"But I did write a check!" I cried out.

"Did you put it in the mail?" he questioned.

63

I wasn't able to hold back my tears any longer. "I wrote the check yesterday, but I haven't mailed it," I confessed. "The money I thought would be in the post office box for us never came. I didn't think one more day would matter on the payment. You know, sometimes the mail takes longer to arrive than it should."

"Why didn't you just tell me the truth?" Kris pressed.

"I'm sorry," I said between sobs. "I can't believe that I didn't tell you the truth."

At that moment, I wanted to dig a hole and crawl inside it. Kris was kind to me, but I knew I had a mess to clean up. Pressure is a crazy thing, yet I knew the Lord was using our situation to mold me. I was also aware that this was my journey to complete, my fight to finish. I would much rather have had Kris come to my rescue than face the mess I had created by not telling the truth. Unfortunately, things don't often turn out the way we would like them to. The next day, I called the warehouse manager myself and confessed that I had lied and had not sent the check at the time I had promised. He forgave me on the phone. I honestly think my confession strengthened our relationship with him.

> "I'm sorry, Mr. Vallotton," the deputy said, "but your cars were not stolen. They were repossessed by the bank."

I learned so much from my failure, and I never want to do that again! I can now say from experience that it is much better to tell the truth in the beginning than it is to clean up a mess that telling a lie leaves behind. When we push through our fear of man, we take a giant step forward.

I wish I could say that we lived happily ever after from that day forward, but actually things got worse. In the midst of that same winter, I woke up in the wee hours of the night just in time to see the red glow of taillights as they bounced down our dirt road, away from our house. I yelled out to Kris, "Call the sheriff's office! I think someone's stolen both our cars!"

Kris grabbed the phone and dialed the number. We waited eagerly for someone to pick up.

"Sheriff's office," a man said in a calm voice.

Kris excitedly told the deputy what had happened to us. "They just drove out of our driveway a few minutes ago!" he shouted.

"I'm sorry, Mr. Vallotton," the deputy said, "but your cars were not stolen. They were repossessed by the bank. You can come down to the station and collect your belongings that were left inside them."

Kris looked at me and asked for an explanation. I could not believe what I was hearing. How could this be happening? Things were tight, but I had paid the car payment before the end of the month. The second car they took had already been paid off and wasn't even worth towing. This was so humiliating. How was I going to get around with three little kids (Jason had been born by then) and no transportation?

Kris assured me that it was going to be all right. He is always the strong rock in the family. All I could do was cry myself back to sleep. The next morning, we got a ride to work and passed our two cars parked at the repo lot right on Main Street. Talk about adding insult to injury! By the end of the day, after paying a late payment and the repo fees, our cars were back in our driveway—but not before half of the town had seen them in the repo lot. That proved to be the winter from hell.

Overcoming Tough Times

Looking back on those days, I can honestly say that I don't know how we survived that winter. But somehow in the years that followed, we managed to keep growing. Our auto parts store was so profitable that in 1988 we decided to sell our auto repair shops and the 76 station so we could focus all our energy on the parts store. We changed suppliers, to a national chain called Big A Auto Parts, and we were thriving. We became one of the top Big A stores in the nation—quite a feat for a mountain store competing against 3,700 other jobbers in much larger cities.

The prophetic word Dick Mills had given Kris many years earlier about God giving him double wisdom for business seemed to be unfolding every day. But Kris's personality has a major weakness: He gets bored really easily. When Crossroad Auto Parts (the name of our auto parts store) finally started to prosper, the challenge of conquering that mountain seemed over. I wasn't bored; I enjoyed the peace and stability. Living without the stress of daily financial pressure was great with me. I am not wired to need a daily battle, but that is not Kris.

> **I am not wired to need a daily battle, but that is not Kris.**

Another dynamic was also playing out in our lives at the same time. Kris was being discovered by the outside world. When Big A executives visited our auto parts store for the first time to sell us on their brand, they could not believe what we had built in the middle of nowhere. After we became a Big A store, they immediately put Kris on their national advisory council. Soon, they were offering us financing to buy or open other auto parts stores. Kris saw this as God funding his dream. Of course, I wanted to be as supportive of him as he had been with my "little house on the prairie" dream. Furthermore, we were business partners and an inseparable team.

Growing Pains

In 1994, we opened our second auto parts store. It was located in Redding, California, and was funded by a loan from Big A Auto Parts. Our Redding store was beautiful. We put tons of time and energy into that location and thought we had struck a gold mine. Remembering the prophetic words that had been spoken over Kris back in Weaverville,

"If you will go into business, I will bless you," I felt as though I was the most blessed woman ever.

Eighteen months later, we purchased another auto parts store in Willows, California, two and a half hours away from Weaverville. It was right in the middle of farm country. The same guy had owned the Willows store for forty years, so it provided us with a whole new set of business lessons. Our new crew worked day and night to make the Willows store look beautiful, but we had misjudged our farm customers. Let's just say that beauty was not on their top ten list of must-haves. They hated change and wanted to keep everything the way it had always been.

> When you are in the midst of this voyage, it is often hard to grasp that God is much more concerned about the voyagers than the voyage itself!

We were learning a very painful lesson the hard way in Willows. Yet Kris was doing what he loved, and he stayed insanely busy running between three different locations. He was trying with all his might to keep all the plates spinning without losing one.

I will uncover more of our business story a little later. For now, I just want to say that life is a journey or voyage that has many ups and downs. I am sure you already have experienced some of those along your way, just as we have. Yet when you are in the midst of this voyage, it is often hard to grasp that God is much more concerned about the voyagers than the voyage itself!

As Christians, you and I agree intellectually with the idea that we are living our lives in a temporal here and now, and then we will live in an eternal forever. We acknowledge that these circumstances in the here and now are molding us and readying us for eternity.

We are often unaware on our journey, however, of how many times God will lead us into situations with the *sole purpose* of forging us into His royal sons and daughters.

SIX

THRIVING IN LACK

I have learned to be satisfied in any circumstance. I know what it means to lack, and I know what it means to experience overwhelming abundance. For I'm trained in the secret of overcoming all things, whether in fullness or in hunger. And I find that the strength of Christ's explosive power infuses me to conquer every difficulty.

PHILIPPIANS 4:11–13 TPT

I f life is a journey or voyage, then truth is an onion, with layer after layer of revelation. It seems as if just about the time you think of yourself as an expert on a subject, you relive it again and realize that there are other lessons to be learned from the same circumstances.

Kris and I experienced this many times in our years as business owners. In this chapter, I want to give you some insights into the relational dynamic that was taking place in our home, and with our children, during that often-treacherous leg of our voyage.

Nearly a decade passed as we hacked our way through the jungle of IRS liens, winter payrolls, employee challenges and all, while trying to raise a family in the woods fifty miles from nowhere. This is where the rubber met the road of sacrifice, the place where our very survival demanded innovation, perseverance and faith in the God we were getting to know. It was during this season of our life that our children were experiencing what it was like to thrive even in times of lack.

Racing Down Life's Slopes

Living with a risk taker is . . . well, risky! When things pan out, the rewards are great. When things go south, you can find yourself in a heap of trouble. Actually, I would rather call the troubles "divine opportunities." Kris and I have had many of those "opportunities" over the years. I shared some of them with you already.

They say that opposites attract. This is absolutely true of Kris and me. If Kris hears the word *challenge*, he is all in. The harder the problem, the more it entices him. That's not me! I want all the facts, and then I take my time calculating all the risk factors. If the risk factors are low, all right. Actually, they have to be really low, and then I am in. It has been this way all our lives. Kris wants to run, and I would rather walk. He would rather experience the thrill, while I would rather look at the scenery.

Our personal dynamics were on full display the first time I took Kris snow skiing. (If you think his water-skiing adventure was funny, wait for it.) I had been on the slopes a few times, and I thought snow skiing would be something Kris would really enjoy. He could go at his own pace and choose his own run.

Did I mention speed? When Kris snow skied, he was all in. It did not matter that he had never snow skied before in his life, or that he had never taken a single lesson. *Listen to my wife?* he asked himself as we got started. *Why do I need to do that?*

Too late anyway! Off he went, flying down the slopes, way out of control, while I was yelling at him, "*Snowplow! Snowplow!*" But why should he listen to me? I am the one who never falls. I survey the land and act accordingly. I am the responsible one in the family. Some may say I am boring, but I like to call it wisdom.

Kris, however, seeks the thrill of the experience, all while thinking about how he can do it better or faster next time. The risk takers have their eyes on one thing—the prize. On his second time up the mountain,

> Kris wants to run, and I would rather walk. He would rather experience the thrill, while I would rather look at the scenery.

Kris got off the ski lift and decided to go down the advanced slope. Mind you, since this man had never snow skied before this day, he had *no idea* how to stop on skis. He took off down the mountain and pushed himself faster and faster with his poles, while I yelled at him from the top of the slope to *stop*!

He just continued his hasty descent while shouting, "*Skier out of control! Skier out of control!*" all the way down the slope. Other skiers hurried to get out of his way. Finally, by some miracle, he got down to the bottom of the hill, where people were lined up to get on the ski lift. The path to the lift was marked by a rope about three feet above the ground. Kris yelled to the lineup, "*Watch out—skier out of control!*"

People moved out of the way just in time to keep him from running right over them. He ducked the rope, then stood up straight just in time to hit the lodge wall with both skis. Of course, the bindings released his ski boots, so he was literally plastered to the wall like a cartoon character.

I skied past him a minute later, not wanting anyone to associate me with this idiot, and whispered, "You're stupid."

71

But Kris peeled himself off the wall in pure hilarity. He could not stop laughing! By the way, this was not his last run of the day. For his next act, he ran into a young girl as he blasted down the mountain. On contact, he held her up in the air, and one hundred yards later he stopped himself by skiing into a snowbank, which buried the poor girl four feet deep in snow. This is our life together!

Dreamers Gotta Dream

Visionaries are driven by their dreams and the thoughts that come to them in the middle of the night. It is all about the drive and the fight to make nothing into something, to tread where one has never gone before. It is all about the "what-ifs" and the "I think I cans" that propel the visionary/dreamer further and further down the path of success. This is all great when everything is going smoothly and there is some history from the past to bank on. But what is a person to do in the beginning, when money is scarce and experience may be limited? This is exactly how it was for Kris and me when we opened up our first business together.

Most people who go into business don't have a nest egg of extra cash stashed away in the bank somewhere. As I shared with you earlier, it took everything that we had to open up our first business. But from the moment we opened our doors, we were really busy. Being busy doesn't always mean that you are making money. In fact, if you don't properly manage your time, money and customer service, you can lose money very quickly.

Because we were so undercapitalized, it was very important that we collect our accounts receivable quickly. The 76 station business was exploding, which meant so were our expenses. Kris was a great automotive technician, and soon word got around about the excellent work we were doing. We started picking up different fleet accounts around town, which made us the busiest shop in Weaverville history. Because of the increase in business, however, we needed more mechanics to keep up with the extra workflow. More mechanics meant more payroll. More payroll meant more matched taxes. More matched taxes took more money. The list went on and on. Growing a business is fun and exciting, but it is always going to involve risk.

Growing a business is fun and exciting, but it is always going to involve risk.

Our cash flow was beginning to dry up really fast with our newfound growth, not to mention the tough winters we were enduring. You can make a profit and still not have enough cash on hand to pay your bills. To keep up with the ever-growing and ever-changing industry, we also needed more equipment than we had. Every single cent we made was being sown back into the business, which made things tight for us at home. (I told you about our cars getting repossessed that winter.) Every other Friday was payday for our crew, and we always made sure that they were paid first, before we took any money out of the business. Even when we did take a paycheck, we wrote it out only for just the amount we needed.

Well, this is how I became the bookkeeper.

Kris began working more and more hours to try to ease the cash flow situation. Many nights, I would bring dinner down to him because he would get so lost in his work that he would forget to eat. Remember, he had already gone through a nervous breakdown, and we did not need that to happen again.

Living hand to mouth was taxing my spirit and my peace, so I began to think of other creative ways I could help out with our finances. At the time, we could not afford a bookkeeper, so Kris was doing the books himself. We had three little kids, and Kris wanted to make sure that I was able to stay home with them. *There must be something I can do to help, even if I'm a stay-at-home mom,* I thought.

I knew that I was good with numbers. I thought that if I started doing the books, it would free up Kris for several hours a day. Then he would be able to work on more cars, which would in turn bring in more money. I shared the idea with him when he got home. He listened to my plan, but he was not convinced that it was the right thing to do.

"I can still take care of the kids and do the books," I said. "I'll set up a home office, and the kids will be right with me. I'm fully capable of doing both!"

I saw the look in his eyes and knew that Kris really didn't want me working, even from home, but he didn't have a better idea. Let me be clear that Kris had no problem with women working outside the home. He just wanted to make sure our kids were always first in our lives.

"We'll try it for a month and see how it goes," he responded.

I can be pretty stubborn, I thought. *I can make this work!* I was not going to fail.

Getting Creative

Sometimes in the midst of life's challenges, you just need to make a game of it. I was determined to win! At that time, there were five of us in our family, plus our two huge dogs (the German shepherd and Irish Setter I mentioned earlier). I decided to allow myself $200 a month for groceries, challenging myself to perform the impossible because there was no way that $200 would cover everything we needed. But I saw it as a great opportunity to test my skills in frugality, organization, perseverance and pure determination.

Flopping myself down on the couch, I started thinking of ways I could stretch my dollar. *Sales!* I thought. That one was obvious. I could purchase the Wednesday paper that had all the food sales for the week. *That's a good start*, I thought to myself. *And what about coupons? I can certainly try those. But this is all basic stuff*, I contemplated. *I need to be more creative than this.*

Another idea popped into my head. If I planned my meals out ahead of time, I could buy food in bulk and get a better price. I could make a monthly dinner menu and purchase the food according to my monthly menu. I went to my computer and began working on

Sometimes in the midst of life's challenges, you just need to make a game of it. I was determined to win!

my newfound idea. I started typing in all our favorite meals, along with side dishes that were paired accordingly. Instead of just filling boxes, I needed to plan a strategic method of nightly dinners. This is where the fun came in! I started to think about chicken and all the entrees you could make with a bird. Baked chicken, chicken fried rice, chicken potpie, chicken soup, chicken noodle casserole . . . *And what about beef?* I thought after that. Pot roast, beef potpie, beef stew, beef soup . . .

I had just made shopping so much easier, not to mention more efficient. No longer did I have to think about what I was going to make for dinner, because the menu was already planned out. I was so proud of myself! When you create something that really works, you just want to share it with everybody. Think of how many trips to the grocery store you could save yourself by working my plan.

What are some other ways I can help bring in more money? I thought with a grin on my face. Once again, I flopped down on the couch and began thinking of fun things I could do. *Energy*, I thought. *How can I cut back on our electric bill? We live in the mountains and have a woodstove. I bet I could cook on top of the woodstove.*

The kids and I made soup and bread rolls that afternoon on the woodstove. Kris came home, and our girls went running up to him before he could even get all the way through the door.

"Daddy, Daddy, look what we made!" they squealed. "It's going to be so yummy!" they both said, jumping up and down.

75

The girls were right. Our dinner was yummy, and not only that, but we also had a ton of fun. That night as Kris and I were in bed, my mind started racing all over the place. *There must be even more that I can do*, I thought. *Think, Kathy, think!*

I must have finally dozed off, because I woke to Kris getting ready for work in the morning. I tried to hurry him out the door so I could pick up my thoughts from where I had left them last night. Once again, I let my mind wander. *Electricity . . . electricity*, I thought. *There's something I'm not seeing clearly yet. . . .*

For months, I had already been lowering the thermostat during the day, when Kris was at work. I never minded a cool house in the winter season, but Kris hated it. He worked all day in the cold air, and coming home to a cold house was the last thing he wanted to do. The kids were dressed warmly and did not seem to mind the lower temperatures, but I would warm up the house a little before Kris got home.

I started looking around our house to see where else I could conserve electricity, and a thought came to me: *Everything electrical is powered through the main circuit breaker box. If I flipped that switch, I would cut power to everything!*

You're probably thinking that I had totally lost it! But remember, these were desperate times, and desperate times called for desperate measures. My next idea was awesome: "Kids, we're going camping!" I said. "Each of you can make your own fort right here in the family room."

Lots of squealing began as the kids turned our furniture on its side and placed blankets on top of it.

"You can't go camping without a lantern," I told them. We had lots of "lanterns" around the house because the power often went out in the winter. I grabbed a few oil lamps, lit them and placed them strategically around the room. I warmed the house with the woodstove and made skewers for the kids out of branches I found outside. Then I gave each of them a few marshmallows to roast. There was lots of laughter, along with sticky fingers. Once our three kiddos finished licking their fingers, they quickly crawled into their tents to "go to sleep."

About ten minutes later, I heard the front door open. "What's going on?" Kris asked in a panicked voice. "Are you guys okay?"

I maneuvered around him as quickly as I could, trying not to run him over.

"Where are you going?" he questioned.

Stepping past him to go outside, I opened the fuse panel and flipped the main circuit breaker, and on came the lights.

By now, Kris was completely frustrated. "Stop right now and tell me what's going on!" he demanded when I came back in.

He walked into the family room, and six eyeballs popped their heads out of their little tents and yelled out, "We're camping, Daddy!"

"What's all this about?" Kris asked me.

"I've been trying to figure out ways to help out financially so that all the pressure doesn't end up on your shoulders. It took some creative thinking, but I've made a few changes to the way I do things at home, and the kids haven't noticed a difference. In fact, they love it! They get to go camping, we read stories by an oil lamp and we even roast marshmallows and hot dogs. I just want to help out wherever I can. It's all good, honey. I really don't mind."

Kris took my hand and pulled me close. Looking into my eyes, he said, "You amaze me every day, Kathy Vallotton! You always look to the positive instead of the negative in any situation you're in, and that's one of the things I love about you."

Lessons Learned

Every day brings new challenges. It's how we roll. As for those hard times, I would never want to go through them again, but I wouldn't run from them either. There are some lessons we can only learn in the midst of the fire. The goal is to learn the lesson and then move on to the next one.

I think of myself as someone in a constant state of learning. It would be pretty scary to think that I have experienced all life has for me. It is even scarier to think that I have learned all the Lord has to teach me. So when I get in the middle of a crazy season, I look at what is lying ahead of me and line my problems up in single file. I cannot tackle everything at once without getting overwhelmed, but I sure can take problems on one at a time.

> I cannot tackle everything at once without getting overwhelmed, but I sure can take problems on one at a time.

The goal is to confront life's challenges without losing your peace. If you find yourself in a situation where darts are flying at you from every direction, take time to stop and focus on Jesus. Put your mind on a short leash and guide it back to the place where you felt God's peace all around you. Then camp out there for a while. If you have lost your peace altogether, ask yourself, *When was the last time I felt Him near me?* Then go back there. Remember this: You may have lost sight of Him, but the Prince of Peace will never lose sight of you.

SEVEN

ANGELS ON ASSIGNMENT

Are they not all ministering spirits, sent out to render
service for the sake of those who will inherit salvation?

HEBREWS 1:14

I love seeing God work miracles among us, as He does so frequently in our lives when we put our faith to the test. I know there are so many times that the Lord intervenes in our situations, even though we are completely unaware of it. God is not a show-off. He does not brag. Some of His most magnificent work, His most beautiful creations, His most stunning inventions, are often hidden inside ugly rocks, locked away in some distant galaxy or buried deep beneath the ocean waters.

Solomon described God's character like this: "It is the glory of God to conceal a matter; but the glory of kings is to search out a matter" (Proverbs 25:2). It is so encouraging when God answers our prayers, but the ultimate display of His love for us is when He does something we never asked for or never even knew we needed. Once in a great while, we catch a sneak peek of His fatherly care for us hidden in some divine act of benevolence that is hardly noticeable.

Board for Life

I caught a glimpse of God's greatness many years ago when He intervened in a life-threatening situation. Beni, our pastor's wife, was having a women's gathering at her house one evening. Kris had just gotten home from work, and I was getting ready to leave for the meeting. I popped my head into the bedroom to let him know that I was leaving, and off I went.

It was a freezing winter night when the kids were still quite young, and there were three feet of snow on the ground. When I finally made it to Beni's house, I got a phone call from Kris. "Do you have Jason with you?" he asked.

"No," I said. "Remember, I told you I was leaving, and I'd see you later, when I got home?"

Frantic, Kris said, "But Jason is gone!"

Jason was only about eighteen months old at the time. We both knew there was no way he could survive the frigid nighttime air outside, let alone the snow on the ground. "I gotta go find him!" Kris yelled into the phone.

We lived on a gravel road that had a sloping incline about two hundred feet long. A creek passed through a large culvert at the bottom of our road. In the summer months, not much water flowed through the creek. But in the winter, it was a different story. Water would flow like a rushing river under the small "bridge" that spanned the two banks. About a month earlier, there had been so much water flowing in the creek that we literally had to pull the culvert out, which left about an eight-foot-wide, four-foot-deep ditch flowing madly out of control between the end of our gravel road and the street. We were not prepared for this at all and could not fix it until the rains had stopped. It was a mess! In order to get to our cars that were parked out on the street, we had to cross the creek by walking across a two-by-six plank that went between our driveway and the street.

We both knew there was no way Jason could survive the frigid nighttime air outside, let alone the snow on the ground.

To make matters even more dire, Jason had disappeared on a pitch-dark, moonless night. Kris told me afterward that he went running frantically out of the house, yelling Jason's name. He ran up and down our long driveway, tromping through the deep snow but not seeing or hearing anything. Then he suddenly remembered that the "bridge" was out. He ran down to the creek, and with only a dim flashlight looked everywhere that he could see.

"*Jason! Jason!*" Kris yelled. Nothing. The water was rushing so hard that he could not hear anything besides the noise of it raging through the creek bed. In a panic, he kept saying, "God, *please, please* help me!"

Kris started to run back up toward the house when he thought he heard a soft whimper coming from the weeds closest to the street. "*Jason!*" Kris screamed. Nothing. Yet as soon as Kris started to run toward the house, the cries started again. He shined the flashlight up the creek one way and down the other side. He could hear something in the bushes, but he could not see anything.

Kris ran across the board spanning the creek, and out of the corner of his eye, he saw something huddled down on the ground. It was Jason! When Jay saw his dad, he began crying even harder.

"Just stay there!" Kris said. "Stay there!" Dodging trees and thick brush, Kris spotted Jason and grabbed him, tears flowing down his face in relief. All he could do was to say, "He's alive! He's alive!"

81

I was just getting ready to race for home when Kris called the Johnsons' house. "I found him!" he proclaimed.

"Where was he?" I asked.

"He must have seen you leave the house and tried to follow you. He got to the bridge and crossed over the creek on the narrow board," Kris responded, still trying to catch his breath.

I was speechless with relief, but my heart also sank at the thought of how close Jason must have come to slipping off that skinny board and falling to his death. The water was rushing so hard that night that there would have been no way he would have survived.

Angels Watching over Me

Every time I think about this story, I flash back to a picture I saw many years ago in a Christian bookstore. It was of two young kids playing on a rickety old bridge that spanned a whitewater river far below. The children were surrounded by angels who were ensuring their safety.

Jesus said that children have angels assigned to them (see Matthew 18:10). I am sure that Jason's angels must have been working overtime that night. Just another miracle in the Vallotton home, taking place right before our eyes.

These are times that you cannot take for granted. You cannot deny the power of God when you see it happening right before your eyes. Just think of how many times God was with us and we never even knew it. We have a good Daddy!

For Lack of Words

Years later, my daughter Jaime walked by my two-year-old granddaughter Mesha's room as Mesha was playing quietly by herself. Seeing that all was well, Jaime left and began to clean up after the morning's breakfast. A few minutes went by, and then Jaime heard some giggling coming from Mesha's room. Curious, she quietly walked over and poked her head inside to see what was happening. As she watched my granddaughter, it was as if Mesha was having a gibberish conversation with nobody. Mesha pointed up into the corner of the room, rocking herself back and forth as she continued to interact with something Jaime could not see. Writing it off as child's play, Jaime went back to her cleaning.

Several weeks later, Jaime was taking a bath and decided to put Mesha in the tub with her. It was not uncommon for my daughter, a busy wife and mom, to try to get a few minutes alone with God each day. *Why not the bathtub?* she thought. *Some of Dad's greatest revelations and visitations from God have happened in the tub!*

> Mesha was being entertained by angels, just like the angel who had been watching over little Jason at the creek.

Several minutes went by, when all of a sudden Mesha jumped up in the tub, looked up in the corner of the bathroom, by the door, and said, "Mommy, the birds! Look at the birds!" (She had a great vocabulary for a child her age.)

Jaime was puzzled. *There isn't anything in the room but us,* Jaime thought. It was then that Jaime felt the sweet presence of the Lord in the bathroom. She felt a heavy peace come over the two of them, and Mesha obviously felt the same thing.

The birds . . . Jaime said to herself. She began thinking several weeks back, to the morning when Mesha had been playing in her room, laughing and giggling at nothing. Yet it was not nothing; it was very much something. She was being entertained by angels, just like the angel who had been watching over little Jason at the creek.

Our children and grandchildren are seeing into the third heaven more than we realize. I believe it is because they have not yet developed the ability to talk themselves out of the experience, discounting what they have seen or blaming it on something they ate the night before. Children take things at face value. Adults tend to set up hurdles to jump over, questioning the reality of an angelic experience and wondering whether or not it was really true. For a child, such an encounter is a matter of fact. We need to become more like children in our walk with God. God is always with us, no matter where we are, no matter what circumstances we find ourselves in.

What Was That?

I was in the sanctuary, waiting for my husband, who had been talking to a few people he had just met. Eager to leave, I was trying hard not to let my impatience show. Sunday mornings start early for us, and we had already stayed for two services. As Kris was wrapping up his conversation, something hit me hard on the back of my shoulder. "Ouch!" I said.

"What's wrong?" Kris asked.

"Who hit me?" I questioned.

"What do you mean?" Kris asked.

"Someone just hit me in the back," I exclaimed.

Looking a bit puzzled, Kris said, "Almost everyone is gone from the sanctuary, and there hasn't been anyone behind you."

The hit was hard, and I could feel the lingering effects of it to my shoulder. My mind was buzzing around, trying to figure out what just happened. I looked over at Kris, hoping he could shed some light on the situation.

Just a split second later, I felt the overwhelming presence of the Holy Spirit come over me. The last thing I remember is dropping to the floor, oblivious to anything that was going on around me. I was gone in the Spirit! I can't tell you what the Lord said to me that day, but I can tell you that His ministering angel comforted me in a way that I had never experienced before. I thought that I was on the floor for just a few minutes, but after talking to Kris, I found out I was down for about thirty minutes. It's amazing how much work the Holy Spirit can do inside each one of us when our mind is disengaged and our spirit is opened up wide!

> I can just imagine an angel saying to the Lord, "Watch this! This will get her attention."

God was trying to get my attention that day, and He got it. I can just imagine an angel saying to the Lord, "Watch this! This will get her attention."

Did I ever see the angel with my eyes? No, but I did feel his touch, and it was very powerful. Can anyone talk me out of what happened that Sunday afternoon? I think not, for I am a woman with an experience and a story to tell.

EIGHT

SIGNS THAT MAKE YOU WONDER

God added his witness to theirs. He validated their ministry with signs, astonishing wonders, all kinds of powerful miracles, and by the gifts of the Holy Spirit, which he distributed as he desired.

HEBREWS 2:4 TPT

Have you ever had an experience that changed your life forever and honestly transformed you from the inside out? I know it's common for people to make statements like "that book changed my life" or "that message really had an impact on me!" But did it really have a lasting effect on your soul, or are you just trying to describe a new perspective you gained on a particular subject?

I am simply trying to point out that in our quest to describe a great experience to someone else, it's common for us to use words that exaggerate the impact that something had on our lives. Yet there are times when you do experience something so impactful, so divinely powerful, that you feel lost for words. It is like trying to explain your first kiss to someone who has not yet experienced puberty, or trying to describe falling in love to your five-year-old. The truth is that some things really cannot be explained; they can only be experienced.

Free-Falling

I had one of those profound, epic experiences back when we were at Mountain Chapel in Weaverville that has forever marked my soul. It all began when the women of Mountain Chapel (the church Bill Johnson pastored for seventeen years before coming to Bethel Church) decided to have a women's retreat. Our leadership team worked on the details for months ahead of time, so we knew we had a great plan. Yet none of us had any idea what God was about to do.

When the time for the retreat arrived, I gathered a few things, packed my bag and got ready to head out the door. I gave Kris a big hug and thanked him once again for taking on the "mom" role for the weekend. When I was bending down to give the kids a kiss, Jason said, "Mommy, what are we going to eat when you're gone?"

I looked into his eyes and said, "I'm sure that your dad has some great surprises for you!"

If the truth be told, one time when I left our daughter Jaime with Kris alone, he gave her black licorice, red licorice (in case she didn't like the black) and two different flavors of ice cream. She was on such a sugar high that when she came off it, she fell asleep in her high chair, with her head in the bowl of melted ice cream.

I shook off my anxiety at that memory and proclaimed, "You guys will survive. Dad knows how to make tuna and eggs, and he can boil soup!" Kris and I both chuckled to ourselves. For the record, Kris cannot cook worth a darn.

We ladies arrived at the retreat center about an hour later, and it was beautiful. The center was tucked away as a large, cozy cabin high in the Trinity Alps. I couldn't think of a place I would rather be with all my girlfriends. We ate, worshiped and had lots of prayer time together throughout the night. The Spirit of the Lord was filling that retreat center with His presence in such a way that I don't have words to describe my experience. Something was happening . . . something really awesome.

> **The Spirit was moving so powerfully that everyone was touched. It was like falling into a river of intense love and deep joy all at the same time.**

The Spirit was moving so powerfully that everyone was touched. It was like falling into a river of intense love and deep joy all at the same time, and we were caught up in the middle of it. Suddenly, we all spontaneously began to sing and dance. It felt as if chains were coming off our arms. Women grabbed streamers and flags and started waving them around as they danced wildly throughout the cabin. The next thing you know, we were all headed out the door.

I looked around to see my friends leaping and dancing, free as birds, worshiping with all their might in the middle of a green, lush meadow. It reminded me of what it must have been like to see King David dancing in the street before the Lord. There was so much freedom and joy. Never before had I ever experienced something so powerful and so freeing at the same time. It was just God and us women playing together in the field, as though we were children.

Sunday morning arrived, and after our weekend away, we left the retreat center changed women. We reached church just in time for the Sunday morning service. Worship began, and the power of God exploded. The women who had gone on the retreat began dancing in the aisles as they waved their flags and streamers. We marched up and down the rows of the church as more and more people joined us. We danced our way around the inside of the theater (the home of Mountain Chapel). If only you could have seen the look on our husbands' faces! They did not really know what to do, but they also did not want it to stop. From that day on, Mountain Chapel became a place of encounter with the Holy Spirit every Sunday. This atmosphere revived the innermost being of nearly everyone who dared to walk through those doors.

The Joy of Friendship

I received the Lord when I was seventeen years old, and my life forever changed. Yet encounters like I experienced at the retreat years later freed me from years of religious performance. Over time, I grew to understand that my relationship with God is a two-way street. Jesus actually wants to spend time with me and enjoys my company. He longs for me to share my heart with Him and be open about my thoughts and feelings.

Before my radical renewal, opening up to God was not an easy thing for me to do because it required me to be vulnerable, intimate and personal with Someone I hardly knew. Little did I realize that God already knows everything about me. He does not need me to check in with Him every day to give Him the latest lowdown on my life as part of a ritual or a to-do list. I used to gravitate toward that kind of structure and performance. I made mental lists of what I thought I was supposed to say to God. I also warred within myself over questions about having a relationship with Him: *Do I just pray for other people? Or do I pray for things that I need? Or should I only recite prayers that are already written?* There was so much to think about, and I wanted to get it right! I often got discouraged because nothing I came up with seemed spiritual enough.

The retreat encounter destroyed my to-do lists, however, and wrecked my paradigm. The Lord just kept saying, *Tell Me whatever is on your heart. It doesn't have to be pretty or eloquent. There doesn't have to be a rhyme or a reason to our talks.*

I had spent years making our relationship really difficult, when He was wanting it to be so natural. The women's retreat opened a door to God that led me into encounter after encounter for years afterward. I learned that God just liked being with me. It was like having a new best friend.

I lost my focus on the congregation and began to feel this overwhelming sense of joy sweep over my soul.

A couple of Sundays after the retreat, I was leading worship in the morning service when I began to feel the presence of the Holy Spirit in the room. I lost my focus on the congregation and began to feel this overwhelming sense of joy sweep over my soul. Have you ever been in a serious moment, and then something funny goes through your mind and you can't stop laughing? It was kind of like that. First, I began giggling just a little bit. I tried to tell myself to stop it, but I could not control the overwhelming feeling of joy that was raging through my body. We were in the middle of worship, but I was acting as if I were watching a comedy at the theater!

Before I knew it, I fell onto the keyboard, with my chest pressing against the top two octaves of keys. I couldn't believe this was happening, but I couldn't stop it. I kept swinging my arms around the front of the keyboard, trying to hit the Off switch, to no avail. The next thing I knew, Pastor Bill came to my rescue and graciously pressed the Off button, ending the resounding sound of combined notes that made no sense to the ear.

I don't remember much of what happened after that, except for Kris holding me up as he tried to get me out of the church and into our car. I thought I would "sober up" when I got home, but nope! I staggered into our house and flopped down onto the couch, feeling so lighthearted and happy. The experience lasted long into the next day. I had never felt anything like that in my life. Kris and I had been through so much turmoil in those years with our struggling business that the joy of the Lord was very much welcome. Nehemiah mirrored my experience when he wrote, "The joy of the LORD is your strength" (Nehemiah 8:10). Joy is actually a weapon the Lord has given us to combat the enemy. It is tormenting for the devil to hang around happy people.

The "Statue of Liberty Anointing"

Not everyone experiences the Lord's presence the same way. We jokingly say that Kris has a classic case of the "Statue of Liberty anointing." In the midst of the renewal that was going on in the 1990s, with people all around us having intoxicating experiences in the presence of God, Kris remained largely untouched. Some people would break out in holy laughter, while others experienced tears as they became engulfed in God's love. Kris felt nothing. Absolutely *nothing*. Yet in the midst of his un-experience, he would pray for people all around him and they would get touched by God in such a powerful way that they often fell on the ground. It was beautiful and yet painful to watch Kris push through his ongoing disappointment at not having such encounters himself.

The truth is that for many years, Kris struggled with thoughts that there was something wrong with him. I can remember when we first got saved and were attending the Cathedral of Faith in the Bay Area. Pastor Kenny Foreman gave an altar call at the end of his message and invited everybody who wanted to experience the power of God to come to the front. I jumped up and practically ran to the altar, while Kris followed some distance behind me. I got in line and waited a little nervously. I was seventeen years old and had never experienced the power of God before.

Finally, I was next in line for ministry. Pastor Foreman looked into my eyes and prayed a short prayer over me, and then *boom*, down on the floor I went. I had no idea that I was going to fall over, but thankfully someone caught me before I hit the floor. The Holy Spirit was surging through my body as if I had grabbed on to a thousand-volt electrical wire. It was such an exhilarating yet peaceful experience all at the same time.

After a few minutes, I sat up and looked around. I didn't see what had happened to Kris. I got up and began walking back to my seat, and then I realized Kris was already there.

"That was amazing!" I proclaimed. "I've never in my life experienced anything like that before. I feel so peaceful. What happened to you?"

Kris replied, "Pastor Kenny looked into my eyes and said, 'You don't want to be here, do you?' I told him not really. He put his hand on my shoulder and prayed a short prayer. When he was done, I graciously thanked him and walked off. I felt so stupid."

When we joined the staff at Bethel Church in 1997, Kris's struggle intensified dramatically because the congregation was in the midst of a great outpouring of the Holy Spirit. They were gathering for services three to five times a week, and Bill and the Bethel teams were emphasizing God encounters in every meeting. Most of the time, this would result in the Holy Spirit moving so powerfully that hundreds of people would literally fall to the floor as they encountered the presence of God. The meetings would go on for hours, often ending in the wee hours of the next morning. Kris was a major part of the ministry team, so he felt a responsibility for the services. But the truth is that the struggle in his soul seemed to intensify as more and more people were touched by the power of the Spirit, while Kris experienced nothing.

I recall a specific time when Kris was so discouraged that I thought he was going to quit and go back into the business world. It happened when John and Carol Arnott spoke at one of our conferences. After

> **The Holy Spirit was surging through my body as if I had grabbed on to a thousand-volt electrical wire.**

they finished their teaching, they had everyone in the conference stand in lines throughout the sanctuary. The Arnotts went down the lines and laid hands on everyone there. God was moving so powerfully that there was literally no one left standing in the entire sanctuary—no one except Kris! Somehow, he ended up in the very middle of the room, standing there all by himself, with *everybody* else on the floor, experiencing Jesus.

During that season, people lightheartedly began to label Kris as "HTR," meaning, "Hard to Receive." It was a playful expression, thrown around to tease him (and a few others), but secretly it was killing Kris. Frankly, although I really felt bad for him, I was not much help because I seemed to be a lightning rod for God's presence. In the midst of Kris's "I don't feel a thing" struggles, I was often the one in the room who was overwhelmed by the Holy Spirit. Many times, I would find myself down on the ground once again, experiencing God's incredible peace in another intense encounter with Him.

"Why do these types of manifestations happen?" you ask. My best guess is that God just likes being with us. He wants us to experience what we cannot explain. I like the way Bill Johnson puts it: "If your relationship with God doesn't have an element of mystery to it, then you have an inferior relationship with Him, because He wants to do *more* than we ask or think."

Jesus also talked about signs and wonders. I am convinced that these experiences are often some of those signs that make us wonder!

It's God's Business

Unfortunately, Kris's journey with God caused those signs to make him wonder if there was some hidden sin in his life, or some spiritual barrier to experiencing the intoxicating presence of the Holy Spirit. In times like this, many Christians reduce their theology to their experience, meaning that they build a theological case for their lack of experience.

I remember a close friend of ours I will call Bob (not his real name) who exemplified this way of thinking. Kris was in a meeting with Bob the day after I fell onto the keyboard, intoxicated in the Spirit. Referring to my experience, Bob boldly proclaimed to the guys in the room that morning, "There is no way God would do something like that. Show me a Scripture that validates being 'drunk' in the Spirit!"

Kris remained quiet. He knew I would never fake a manifestation, but he was having his own theological concerns with my experience. A few days later,

> **Many Christians reduce their theology to their experience, meaning that they build a theological case for their lack of experience.**

Sunday morning rolled around and we were all passionately singing together as I led worship. All of a sudden, Bob fell down on the floor of the theater as if he were struck by lightning. He shook violently under the power of the Holy Spirit, banging his knees against the chairs that were bolted down to the slanted floor of the theater.

Kris was sitting a few rows behind Bob. He got up and stood over him and proclaimed, "I don't know if this is God, Bob. . . . Show me a Scripture for your experience!"

Bob, still vibrating like a cartoon character who had grabbed a bare electrical cord, looked up from the floor and blurted out, "Shut up, Vallotton!"

I think Kris would have mirrored Bob's initial approach to these manifestations if I had not been one of the first people to get "holy wrecked" by God. But we have been together since I was twelve years old, and Kris could see that I was being transformed from the inside out. He was actually excited for me, and he encouraged me to press into my experiences with God.

At the same time, my encounters with Jesus thrust Kris into a catch-22 situation. He knew these manifestations were from the Lord, but he was not having them himself, and he struggled to reconcile all of this with the Scriptures. (One thing people might not know about Kris is that the guy is a Bible nut. He reads his Bible all the time, and he is vigilant about things being "scriptural.")

As time passed, Kris began to get revelation from the Scriptures that validated my experience (and that of many others). He could see that many people in the Bible had powerful experiences with God that often resulted in some awkward manifestation in their bodies. Daniel fell down and shook like a leaf when he encountered God (see Daniel 10:8–10). At the dedication of Solomon's Temple, the glory of the Lord showed up as a cloud that resulted in the priests being unable to stand up in His presence (see 2 Chronicles 5:11–14). Ezekiel had a crazy experience in which the Spirit of God grabbed him by the hair and thrust him through the midheaven (see Ezekiel 8:1–4). In Acts 2:1–13, the Holy Spirit was poured out on a bunch of people, resulting in something like "tongues of fire" as the people spoke in tongues (verse 3). Onlookers who were watching the outward expression of the Holy Spirit's outpouring on the disciples described it as making the disciples look drunk on alcohol. When the apostle John encountered Jesus Christ, he fell down like a dead man (see Revelation 1:17).

A relationship with God isn't a one-size-fits-all!

The biblical stories go on and on, making it very clear that the result of God showing up in the midst of people often looks confusing or even strange. In fact, look at a few of the adjectives used to describe the people who witnessed the events in the Acts 2 outpouring of the Spirit. They were *thunderstruck, confused, their heads were spinning,* and *they couldn't make head or tail* of anything they were hearing (see verses 5–13 MESSAGE).

I tried to help Kris work through his agony on the issue. "A relationship with God isn't a one-size-fits-all!" I exhorted. "God speaks differently to you than He does to me. Besides, you know things about people that are crazy amazing," I said. "I wish that I could hear from God the way you do." (I will talk more about his prophetic gifting later in the book.)

The truth was, no matter what I said, it never seemed to put Kris's heart to rest. Then finally, some years later, God answered Kris's dilemma when he was seeking the Lord again about his struggles with the whole situation. The Lord said to Kris, *It's none of your business how I choose to touch people. When I touched Solomon, he got smart, and when I filled Samson with My Spirit, he got strong. When My Spirit fell on Elijah, he became fast and could outrun chariots, yet when I filled Bezalel with My Spirit, he became a great artist and craftsman. Stop comparing the way I touch others to your own experience! I will manifest in and through you the way I choose. Just be open to My work in your life and don't build cases against people who experience Me differently. I am the Lord in the midst of My people, and I know how to reach the heart of everyone who is willing to allow Me to move in their lives!*

I want to encourage you that no matter what you have experienced in God already, there is more! He has so many encounters just waiting for you. God's Spirit on your life might look different than it does on other people's lives, just as it looks very different between Kris and me. But the way you encounter God will be just what you need in order to grow in Him. Press into Him, and He will meet you there.

NINE

MIRACLES AND MANIFESTATIONS

For when you saw me hungry, you fed me. When you found me thirsty, you gave me something to drink. When I had no place to stay, you invited me in, and when I was poorly clothed, you covered me.

MATTHEW 25:35–36 TPT

D o you really know what it is like to live a life where miracles happen all around you? Real miracles? It is easy to say "that was a miracle" about something in a flippant sort of way, using those words like a common phrase, without thinking about the true meaning of the word *miracle* or how it has really had an impact on your life or the lives of others. But it is quite another thing to be living in these God moments of life, never knowing what is going to happen next. The quest for miracles will often drive you to your knees, where you find yourself facedown on the ground in furious prayer. This is our story as a family. It is in the Vallotton DNA—part of the inside scoop about the drive we have as a family to see God move powerfully in us, to us and through us.

One of the most powerful lessons we learned early on as a family is that miracles are commonly discovered in "the land of risk," and there are few things riskier than inviting strangers into your home to live with you. In the first eighteen years of our marriage, our guests often outnumbered our own children. This dynamic thrust us into the adventure of a lifetime, where there was never a dull moment at the Vallotton home.

> One of the most powerful lessons we learned early on as a family is that miracles are commonly discovered in "the land of risk."

So much of our passion to touch the homeless, help the broken and free the captives was inspired by a radical young Jesus Freak named Tracy Evans. We met her when she was a newly saved eighteen-year-old riding a motorcycle to our church in Weaverville. Tracy is the most courageous and outrageously evangelistic Christian we have ever known. Kris and Jason actually wrote a book about her titled *Outrageous Courage* (Chosen, 2013). Tracy notoriously roamed the streets at night to look for lost people she could lead to the Lord. She would spend time with them, share the love of God and then take them to her tiny little bungalow apartment and tuck them in for the night, ending up on our couch herself. This went on for years.

One of the greatest miracle moments in Vallotton family history began when Tracy came home one day from work and began telling me about a girl she had met whom I will refer to as "Sharon" (not her real name). Tracy was working as a nurse at the local hospital, where she met Sharon. Tracy went on to explain to me that Sharon had ended up in the hospital because she was all cut up from running into some sharp pieces of trash in the dark. (There was a lot more to that story, none of it good.) She had no family to speak of, and on top of all that, it was her birthday.

"Do you think you can bake a cake for my new friend?" Tracy asked. "I'd like to bring it to her house. She's getting out of the hospital today, and I think she's all alone."

Sharon's situation touched me deeply. I felt sorry for her, and compassion gushed out of me like an untamed river.

"Sure!" I spoke up. "I'd love to help any way I can."

A few hours later, Tracy and I packed up the kids, jumped in my car and drove off to deliver a birthday cake to her newfound friend. We finally arrived at Sharon's place, which was a beat-up old bus in the midst of an auto junkyard.

"This is the place," exclaimed Tracy enthusiastically. "Come on, let's get out!"

Frankly, that was the last thing that I wanted to do, but Tracy jumped out of the car ahead of me. I grabbed the cake and told the kids to lock the car doors.

As we reached the bus, Tracy knocked on the door. No one answered. *Good*, I thought, *there's nobody home.* "Let's just leave the cake and get out of here," I said sheepishly.

"Let me look inside," Tracy insisted.

"No! No!" I insisted. "We could go to jail for breaking into someone's house."

"Well," Tracy said, "this isn't exactly a house, and the door is unlocked."

I found myself walking in right behind Tracy as she squeezed through the tiny door and put the cake on the table. "Okay, we did it," I said. "Now let's get out of here!"

The place was a mess, and I felt as though I had just walked into some dark backwoods scene from a horror movie. My soul was ravaged with terrible thoughts as I imagined some evil man lurking in the shadows, grabbing us from behind and dragging us into a field to kill us.

I hurried back to the car, with Tracy in tow. As we were driving away, I looked right at her and said, "Tell me *exactly* why Sharon ended up in the hospital, and don't skimp on any of the details! Who is this lady, and how did you get involved with her?"

"I already told you about the junk that she ran into last night," Tracy answered. "All the people in town call her the Amazon Woman because she goes to the bars, has a few drinks, turns into an animal and beats up anyone who gets in her way. She's been involved in satanism, and she's really confused. What she needs is a secure, loving family to live with for a while," Tracy calmly explained.

Kris came home just as Tracy finished telling me Sharon's story. "Hey, girls, how was your day?" he inquired.

Without hesitation, Tracy recapped the story for him. "What she needs now is a good home to stay in, just for a while," Tracy insisted. "Can she please stay with you for a few days?" she pressed. "I know it would really make a difference in her life, and she probably won't be around during the day much since she works."

"I don't know about that," I interrupted. "I need to talk this over with Kris."

Later that evening, I got Kris alone and explained my concerns. "We have little kids," I said. "I just don't know if our home is the best place for Sharon." We talked into the wee hours of the morning and finally both agreed that she could stay with us for one week at the most.

Miracles on Repeat

Anytime someone moves into your home, there is an adjustment period, but I could see that this time around was going to be a *big* adjustment. Kris and I decided that Sharon would sleep on our couch downstairs instead of staying upstairs with the girls. We wanted to make sure we could keep an eye on her at all times.

When she finally arrived at our house, we were a little shocked. She was six feet tall and had long, dark hair with a couple of white streaks running through it. She was built like a man and looked like a biker mama.

This is going to be a little scarier than I anticipated, I concluded to myself. The one redeeming thing I noticed right away was that Sharon was really good with the kids. She had a child who was no longer living with her and whom she missed a ton. She would often tell us stories about their time together. As I watched her interact with my girls, I could see that they were filling some of the void left in her heart by her child's absence.

I also discovered in those first few days that Sharon was streetwise but had very little in the way of common sense or family values. She knew nothing about modesty or integrity. In fact, I don't think those were even in her vocabulary. I concluded that I was going to have to put on my big-girl pants, because this lady needed me to show her some good, strong, motherly love.

> I was going to have to put on my big-girl pants, because this lady needed me to show her some good, strong, motherly love.

"Sharon," I said, "you can't walk around the house barely dressed! Your pants are falling off your butt, and everything that shouldn't be showing is showing!"

"Nothing I have fits anymore," she fired back. "I have nothing else to wear."

I grabbed the sewing machine out of the laundry room and began trimming, hemming and altering every piece of clothing Sharon had to her name. When she tried on her newly altered clothes, she looked like a new person. I could tell that there was a bit of pride coming back into her eyes. Sadly, all her life she had only been exposed to lust, lies and destruction. My simple act of service was already beginning to restore her dignity.

Days turned into weeks, and weeks turned into months as Sharon slowly integrated into our family. She was learning about the love of God and was experiencing miracles right in front of her eyes. For instance, one day Shannon, my youngest daughter, caught her finger on something sharp that dug into her skin, and she began to bleed all over the floor. Sharon saw it happen and started yelling for help.

"Hold her hand under the faucet," I told Sharon as I formed a really quick *Jesus, stop this bleeding* prayer over Shannon's hand. Then I went to find some bandages to wrap around her finger.

Suddenly I heard Sharon yelling at me, "*It's gone!* I can't find a cut anywhere on her hand! What did you do to her?"

"I didn't do anything, but it looks as if Jesus did," I responded. (I was a little surprised myself, actually.) These kinds of supernatural acts repeated themselves over and over in the time while Sharon lived with us. It was impossible to live in our house in those days and not believe in miracles. We saw the raw power of God displayed nearly every day in our home. Sometimes it was a dramatic incident, and other times it was just a simple act of benevolence.

The Rest of the Story

Sharon lived with us for months, and all of us were changed by the transforming power of God's love evident in her life. She became a different person during her time in our home, but sadly, a while later she turned back to her old life and got lost in darkness.

It is really hard to watch someone whom you poured your life into and loved so deeply go back to the cesspool of hell. It is a mystery to me how people can experience the transforming love and power of God and then ever go back to their old ways, but the truth is that it happens.

I have learned that one of the side effects of a life of miracles is disappointment. Disappointment not so much because the miracle you are believing for does not take place (although that certainly happens at times), but more often because the people who experience a bona fide act of God don't always change. I have heard it said many times that if everyone in the world could just experience Jesus for themselves, they would turn their life over to Him. This sounds right—and frankly it should be—but the sad fact is that it is not true. Think about it: One-third of the angels who lived with God in heaven and experienced His power, glory and majesty ultimately rebelled against Him.

And then there was Judas, who walked with Christ for three and a half years, observing the miracles He performed on a regular basis as He went around turning water to wine, raising the dead, cleansing lepers, multiplying food and healing the sick. Yet when it was all over, Judas betrayed Jesus for a lousy thirty pieces of silver.

"Why?" you ask. "How could he betray a man so full of love and so obviously the Son of God?"

I have no idea, but it happened. And the truth is, it still happens. Betrayal happens every day, and it happens to my family and me. Frankly, it will happen to you, too, if you love people deeply enough, walk in real power often enough and reach out to the broken frequently enough. You, too, will be betrayed.

> Every time we reach out toward someone in love, we are making a difference in his or her life, whether we see the fruit of it or not.

We have truly lived a life of miracles, but here is the inside scoop, the rest of the story: We have also experienced more than our share of betrayal, heartbreak and disappointment. It is all part of the risk of a radical life of following Jesus. Such disappointment is often involved in the untold story of ministry, hidden behind the curtain with the happy face logo, whispered in secret among only the closest of friends.

Yet in the midst of the disappointment that comes from taking a risk is the joy that comes from loving people right where they are. Jesus was our greatest example of God's love being poured out without expecting anything in return. Some of us plant, some water and others are there for the harvest. Every time we reach out toward someone in love, we are making a difference in his or her life, whether we see the fruit of it or not.

Personally, I love the fact that God wrote about the human failures of His closest followers in the Bible. We read in Scripture about Abraham's lying, David's adultery, Solomon's disastrous last years of kingship, Peter's denial . . . it's all there in black and white for everyone to read for themselves. This is the good, the God and the ugly of a life in Jesus.

TEN

TERRIFIED

Do not yield to fear, for I am always near. Never turn your gaze from me, for I am your faithful God. I will infuse you with my strength and help you in every situation.

ISAIAH 41:10 TPT

Raising kids in a mountain community of three thousand people makes for a powerful bonding experience in itself. But when our kids were young, a group of us from Mountain Chapel decided to start a Christian school. Called Trinity Christian School, it went from preschool through eighth grade. Attendance averaged about forty kids a year, which gave it the feel of a one-room schoolhouse out of the early pioneer days of the Wild West, where kids in multiple grades learned together from a single teacher (although we employed as many as three full-time teachers most years).

Our goal was simple. We wanted to separate our kids from the humanistic values taught in the public school system, and instead educate them in a Christ-centered environment, at least through their forma-tive years. Looking back, I think we may have only just succeeded at covering the bases academically, but I know we excelled at bonding as a community and teaching our kids to love one another!

The one thing I will say is that the school created a heck of a lot of work for us parents! Every one of us worked hard to make sure our children were not missing out on the social dynamics provided by the public schools that we competed with. Those schools had much bet-ter funding for their programs, whereas at our school all the parents pitched in to coach the athletic teams or teach cheerleading or chaperone various social events.

The year Jason graduated from Trinity Christian, Kris and I were commissioned to lead the graduating class of ten teenagers on their eighth-grade extravaganza—a trip to Santa Cruz Beach Boardwalk about five hours away. One of our friends lent us a fifteen-passenger van so all the kids could ride together in one vehicle. I had arranged for us to stay at my in-laws' house for a couple of days. I have to tell you that ten eighth graders staying in a house that was only eleven hundred square feet was, well, insane! What was I thinking? Call me a martyr or call me stupid; I'm not sure which! The house did have a pool, but I don't know if that helped or just added to the chaos. But those couple of days did prove to be everything that the kids dreamed they would be.

> Ten eighth graders staying in a house that was only eleven hundred square feet was, well, insane! What was I thinking?

At the end of the second day, we packed up the kids and headed home. Everyone was tired, which made the trip home noticeably quieter than the ride there. Kris drove, I read and the kids were talking quietly as they shared their most daring ride or bragged about how many times they had ridden the roller coaster without throwing up. There was no texting or playing games on cell phones, since this was a little over 25 years ago. The only cell phones available looked like something out of a Dick Tracy movie—big, bulky, expensive and definitely not game-worthy.

We drove for several hours before the kids finally needed a bathroom break. Kris spotted a service station ahead, so we pulled off the freeway and got gas. The kids jumped out of the van, ran to the bathroom and did their thing. Of course, they all made sure they grabbed chips and soda for the rest of the trip home, to try to satisfy their bottomless appetites. The kids all made their way back to the van, and we counted heads to make sure no one would be left behind. We left the station and made our way back onto the freeway.

It was about 6:00 p.m., and we had been on the road again for only about ten minutes when I noticed an old pickup truck tailgating us. I started to feel uncomfortable and asked Kris to move over into the slow lane. A few seconds later, the driver honked his horn and motioned with his arm for us to pull over.

My first thought was that Kris must have left the gas cap off the van when he filled up, or maybe one of our tires was going flat, because the guy seemed pretty insistent. Just then, he changed lanes and pulled up next to our van. I could see his face, and as I stared at him, I could tell that there was something very wrong . . . there was something about his eyes. They were like nothing I had ever seen before. His eyes turned blood red as he tried to hold my gaze. It was in that moment that I realized I was not looking into the eyes of a man, but a monster.

"Don't pull over! Don't pull over!" I yelled at Kris. Just then, the man's old white Chevy truck pulled in behind our van and tried to ram us from behind. By now the kids were scared, not understanding what was taking place.

I looked over at Kris, and he was holding it all together, calm as can be, as he tried to comfort the kids by telling them everything was going to be all right. He sped up a bit to get away from the truck, but all of a sudden the old truck found a burst of power and moved to the side of our van. With a hard jerk to the right, the truck thrust over into our lane as the man tried to run us off the road. If it had not been obvious what he was trying to do before, it definitely was obvious now. I looked back at the kids, making sure that they had their seat belts on. Several of the girls were crying.

I was doing everything in my power not to lose it myself. "Hold on," I said. "We're going to be okay."

But things were not okay. In fact, they were far from okay! By this time, the people in traffic behind us could see what was happening, and a few brave drivers tried to pull up next to us to keep the man from running us off the road, but their efforts were to no avail. The man in the truck got around them every time. Just when we thought he was going to take another run at us, he passed us and sped off.

"Thank You, Jesus! He's gone," I said. No sooner were those words spoken when he slowed way down and slammed on the brakes right in front of us, nearly causing us to crash into his truck's rear end. Swerving, Kris did everything he could to avoid hitting the guy as we came to a complete stop. Other drivers then stayed several hundred yards behind us, moving forward only as we moved.

By now, I was completely undone! But I was an adult, not a child, and I shouldn't have been acting like a scared kid. I guess I missed that lesson. Just then, I saw the man's backup lights in front of us. He hit the gas pedal and was flying backward toward us! Then he stopped on the right shoulder of the road, and we stopped behind him. He got out of his truck and started running toward us.

The kids in our van began screaming, "He has a gun! He has a gun!" Kris waited until the guy got about ten yards from us, then he hit the gas pedal and swerved around him. Kris sped up to over 100 miles per hour for the next several minutes in an attempt to lose the guy! Soon it felt as if we had indeed lost him.

As we sped off, I begged Kris to take an off-ramp so we could get help. The problem was that the area we were in was so rural that there was nothing around us.

Unbelievably, one of the boys began to yell out, "Here he comes again!" This nightmare repeated itself over and over. Jason and Andy, my son's best friend, did an amazing job at helping keep things as calm in the back of the van as they could. In the front, I was the one who needed help!

O God, if we only make it through this alive! I prayed. Just as that thought went through my mind, another driver pulled up beside us and motioned that he was going to pull over and call 911. Coming up to an exit, he took the off-ramp and disappeared from our sight. At this point we were already about thirty minutes into the chase, and the whole scene would have made a great movie. Sandra Bullock had nothing on us! We were living an experience that people pay good money to watch on TV, but we didn't know how it was going to end and there had been no preview.

> **We were living an experience that people pay good money to watch on TV, but we didn't know how it was going to end and there had been no preview.**

We were approaching a town called Willows (where Kris and I would buy another auto parts store years later) when I saw a couple of cars pulled over on the side of the freeway. "*Wait, it's a cop!*" I yelled out. "Pull over, Kris! Please pull over!" I said in a frantic voice. I rolled down the window as Kris slowed the van, and I screamed at the cop, "*Please help us! He's trying to kill us!*"

The poor officer didn't know what to do. Here was a crazy woman hanging out the van window, screaming something about being killed, while traffic was backed up for half a mile, moving all over the place as if the drivers were scrambling to stay out of the way. I looked back at the officer as we passed him by, just in time to see him leave the guy he had pulled over sitting all by himself. The patrolman ran back and jumped into his car.

Kris moved over into the center median to wait for the cop. Just then, one of the boys yelled, "Watch out! That crazy guy is breaking in!"

The other driver had stopped nearby and had hopped out of his white truck, and now he was hanging onto our van. With his hand through the window, he was trying to unlock the door. Kris threw the van in reverse and dragged the man back and forth, trying to keep him from opening the door. All of a sudden, Kris looked back and realized that he had almost plowed into the California Highway Patrol car. The boys unbuckled their seat belts and grabbed a tire iron they found on the rear floorboard. One of them took a swing at the guy's hand, trying to make him let go.

It was an unbelievably chaotic moment that Kris and I remember a little differently, but I know that the very next words I heard were the officer's: "*Stop*, or I *will* shoot you!"

The barrel of his gun was pointed not at the other driver, but through my passenger window, aimed right at Kris. I yelled at the officer, "*Stop, stop! You have the wrong guy!*"

Kris, confused, tried to tell the cop with the gun trained on him that he had it all wrong. This just made the officer more determined. Using some colorful language, he kept ordering Kris to get out of the vehicle. I was losing it, and I begged my husband just to do as the officer was saying.

"Get out of the vehicle with your hands up!" he commanded again. I looked up at the officer to plead for my husband, when suddenly, out of what seemed like nowhere, we were completely surrounded by what looked like something out of a Jack Reacher movie, complete with lights flashing and a chopper swarming above us, which actually came to rest in front of our van.

The officer at our window yelled at Kris once again, "Get out *now!*"

Just then, I heard the hammer of the pistol click back as the officer stepped closer. Kris threw the van into Park and opened up his door. He came out of the vehicle with his hands in the air and his mouth shut. Two officers who had just arrived at the scene grabbed him, threw him down to the ground and slapped some handcuffs on him.

This can't be happening! I thought. Just then, an officer opened my door and asked if I was all right. "I'll be fine," I said, "but the kids are beyond scared!"

One by one, the officers began helping each of the kids out of the van. They huddled the kids into a small group and started questioning them about why they were in the van and what their relationship was to the driver. By the time they had questioned each of them, the cops realized that they had the wrong guy in cuffs.

I looked up just in time to see one of the officers bringing the guy who had been driving the old truck over to our van. Thankfully, they had detained him as well when they had surrounded the area. The guy was pretty disoriented.

"Point out your daughter," the cop demanded.

Point out your daughter? I said to myself. *What's he talking about?*

One by one, the man looked over the girls. "She isn't here. They must have done something with her!"

As one officer took the man over to the patrol car, another officer came over to Kris and me and told us that the driver of the old truck believed that we had kidnapped his daughter.

"I'm sorry, Mr. Vallotton," this patrolman said, setting him free. "The initial officer on the scene assumed that your wife was the man's daughter. He only had a few seconds to make a quick assessment of the situation. All things pointed toward you being a kidnapper. By the time he realized that he might have been incorrect, other drivers had started getting out of their cars so they could testify to what they had just witnessed."

The other driver was soon taken to jail, and we were left with a van full of scared but very thankful kids who could not wait to get home.

At 6:00 a.m. the next morning, I was awakened out of a sound sleep by our phone ringing.

"Hello, is this Mrs. Vallotton?" asked the voice on the other end of the phone.

"Yes, it is," I replied. "Who is this?"

"I'm the officer who was going to arrest your husband. May I please speak to him?" the voice asked.

I put the phone down and woke Kris up. "Kris! Kris! It's the officer from yesterday, wanting to talk to you." Kris took the phone.

"Mr. Vallotton, how are you doing?" asked the officer.

"I'm fine," Kris replied.

"Well, I'm not," the officer said. He related how he hadn't gotten any sleep, disturbed at the thought of nearly hurting Kris during the incident. The officer was crying as he told his side of the story. "I pulled back the hammer of my gun," he said, "and just before I pulled the trigger to take you down, I heard something inside me say *NO!*"

> "Peace be with you. There will be no loss of life, and I have everything under control."

It was then that the officer knew something wasn't right, and he told Kris he had been on the police force for over twenty years and had never had anything like that happen to him before. "I just wanted to call you today and make sure you were all right," he finished.

"I knew things would work out fine," Kris said. "When the whole ordeal began, the Lord spoke to me and said, *Peace be with you. There will be no loss of life, and I have everything under control.* So I had total peace throughout the whole situation. You couldn't have killed me, because God was protecting me!" Kris reassured him. "By the way, what was wrong with the guy who tried to kill us?"

The officer couldn't give us the details about the man, but he did say, "You already know that he thought you had kidnapped his daughter. When he woke up this morning, he couldn't believe what he had done."

Kris thanked the officer and hung up the phone. We never did hear what happened to the man after that. We assume he must have plea-bargained his sentence, since we never heard from the officer again.

Thoughts That Matter

Kris and I had very different experiences in the same van that day because his soul was at peace and I was terrified. And although he kept reaching over to me during the entire ordeal to comfort me, I refused to be consoled. Instead, I chose to believe fear's facts over Kris's truth. Fear was a better salesman that day, and I purchased its kryptonite at the price of my peace.

After that ordeal, I determined that I would learn from my mistakes, and I tried to choose courage from then on. Yet I struggled with PTSD for a long time afterward. I panicked anytime someone drove too close to me on the freeway. My eyes were constantly looking in my rearview mirror as my mind replayed the chase scene over and over again. As time passed, I realized I was fueling the fire of fear with my own thoughts. My soul was stuck in a rut that kept drawing me back into fear.

> I began to think of "good thoughts" as soldiers on a peacekeeping mission, ready to fight for me at my beck and call.

One night when I was reading my Bible, I suddenly realized that I have power over fear. It was not as though I had not known the Scriptures before that. I had! But in that moment, 2 Corinthians 10:5 became so real to me. It says that we are to be "taking every thought captive to the obedience of Christ." I could see clearly now that I had not taken my thoughts captive. In fact, it was I who was their captive!

115

How do I actually change my mind, get free and find peace? I read another Scripture, Philippians 4:8–9:

> Finally, brethren, whatever is true, whatever is honorable, whatever is right, whatever is pure, whatever is lovely, whatever is of good repute, if there is any excellence and if anything worthy of praise, dwell on these things. The things you have learned and received and heard and seen in me, practice these things, and the God of peace will be with you.

I began to think of "good thoughts" as soldiers on a peacekeeping mission, ready to fight for me at my beck and call. I viewed "bad thoughts" as an army of robbers and murderers trying to steal my peace and kill my joy. I learned quickly that I could deploy my good soldiers through divine meditation on God and His Word. When I considered the attributes of my "good thoughts," I was readying my soldiers for war. And when I considered the impact that those "good thoughts" were having on my soul, I was unleashing my soldiers and commissioning them to destroy hell's effects. But I had to learn to discipline myself to summon the right soldiers, which proved a little more difficult than I anticipated. Sometimes I would get confused and summon both the good and the bad. Consequently, a war would break out on the battlefield of my mind, resulting in a ton of anxiety in my soul.

Other times, it helped for me to imagine my mind as a canvas and my thoughts as "artists." Good thoughts were wonderful artists that painted beautiful portraits of peace on the canvas of my mind, while bad thoughts were "vandals" that spray-painted appalling graffiti on the walls of my imagination. I was the agent of my own transformation because my willpower was the key that determined whom I was authorizing to paint each day, and what kind of painting I was commissioning in the halls of my inner person. I also came to understand that the vandals were often not just my thoughts, but the thoughts of the enemy. Stopping them from defiling my imagination therefore became spiritual warfare in which I had to arrest them, like a police officer incarcerating a criminal who is resisting arrest.

Let me give you a practical illustration of the battle I faced on a daily basis. I could be going down our stairs toward our family room, and I would think, *I better turn on the light because there could be a rattlesnake coiled up on the last step.* Or I could be riding my horse Dreamer and think, *I better not go too fast, because he could spook and jump to the right and I would go flying off.*

Now, you probably realize that both situations could really happen. So where is the balance in the Philippians passage? The Merriam-Webster dictionary defines *meditation* as "contemplation" or "reflection," with the transitive verb *meditate* meaning "to reflect" or "to ponder." I was doing this all the time, but it was in the negative sense, not the positive. It is wise to be cautious and aware, but I was crossing the line and had opened up the door to fear. I was choosing fear instead of faith. I was looking at the negative instead of the positive. But most of all, instead of hearing Jesus, I was giving the enemy an opportunity to speak to me.

Now when I am riding my horses, I purposefully craft my thoughts around what a great ride I will have. I am aware that I am riding a twelve-hundred-pound animal that has a mind of its own. I also think of all the times Dreamer has taken such good care of me in scary situations. They say that animals can sense fear in a person. Your fear can actually be transferred not only to other animals, but to other people. When I have been meditating on the things that are good and pure, inevitably my rides are so much better. Not only do I have more confidence in my horse, but my horse also has more confidence in me.

The Choice Is Yours

Fear or faith? Faith or fear? The choice is yours and mine. They cannot both exist at the same time. The Lord spoke to Kris right as the car chase started, and Kris chose to believe only one thing: *Peace be with you. No harm shall come to any of you.* He did not let fear feed into the situation, but he chose to believe God's word to him over the problem.

Fear or faith? Faith or fear? I know what I need to work on! It's a choice, and I am going to work on making the right one. How about you? Take control of your mind and what you meditate on, and craft a new destiny for your life.

> **Fear or faith? Faith or fear? The choice is yours and mine.**

I want to leave you with a portion of the charge God gave to Joshua in the middle of the toughest season of his life: "This book of the law shall not depart from your mouth, but you shall meditate on it day and night, so that you may be careful to do according to all that is written in it; for then you will make your way prosperous, and then you will have success" (Joshua 1:8).

ELEVEN

LIFE IS ONE BIG ADVENTURE

Trust in the Lord and do good; dwell in the land and
enjoy safe pasture. Take delight in the Lord, and
he will give you the desires of your heart.

PSALM 37:3–4 NIV

What is it like being married to a risk taker? Life is one big adventure! They say that opposites attract, and we all know this statement is true. Whatever Kris is, I am the opposite most of the time. Kris's life runs on adrenaline. Mine runs on peace. I sleep like a baby. Kris . . . well, let's just say his mind never stops turning. He is like the Energizer Bunny. He just keeps going and going. It doesn't matter if it's day or night. Kris is always off to the next big thing, wheels spinning and ready to engage at just the right time. I really admire people who are made the way he is. It just doesn't work for me.

Adventure looks different to different people. I believe that past experiences have a lot to do with the way you look at your future. Two of my kids are wired just like their father, ready to jump all in at a moment's notice. Shannon, who is a spitting image of me, is

Adventure looks different to different people.

very calculated and methodical. She is not a risk taker, and she loves to play it safe. Neither one of us needs change in our daily routine, let alone adding something that has an element of risk.

That is why one night I was surprised when our girls returned home from youth group and said they both wanted to go on a mission trip to China. *Wow*, I thought, *I never saw that one coming.*

"Since when have you had an interest in going to China?" I asked them.

"Several of our friends are going, and we both think it would be a great experience for us," Jaime exclaimed.

"We would be the first from our family ever to travel so far away," Shannon chimed in. "We really want to go!"

Most every summer, Bill Johnson's brother, Bob, took kids on a mission adventure somewhere around the world. This year, the destination was China. I have to admit, I was really leery about letting my girls go so far away without us, but they were pretty persuasive. They soon had both Kris and me talked into letting them go.

"Dad, Mom, it's going to be the trip of a lifetime!" they said.

I don't know if that last statement was supposed to make us feel guilty or more secure. Their persuasive words did not seem to change anything about my feelings, but we found ourselves saying yes to their big adventure.

Jaime and Shannon, along with a few of their friends, spent their next few weeks raising support. They did everything from draining their savings accounts to babysitting to writing support letters, until they had all their finances covered. I have to say, Kris and I were really proud of them. They were working extremely hard for an experience that would last only two weeks, and then be over. I could see that for the girls, however, the preparation was turning out to be just as important as the destination. There is something about having to work hard for what you want in life.

We have always taught our kids that work and integrity are extremely important, and that they should not expect a handout in life. If people were willing to invest in the girls going on the mission trip, they needed to be good stewards of that deposit. "Someone worked hard for the money that will send you off on your adventure," we said. "Don't let them down!"

The big day arrived, and with lots of tears and hugs, our girls walked out the front door, ready to take on their new adventure. "Don't forget to call home!" I yelled as they were rounding the corner.

What have we said yes to? I asked myself as they disappeared from sight. *They are truly in God's hands now. This is going to be the longest two weeks of my life!*

The girls had been gone for two days, and life was happening all around us, as usual. We left our house for work, trying not to think about the girls being so far away. As we walked into our parts store, we were greeted by Kris's brother, Kelly, who also worked for us.

"Good morning!" Kelly said.

"Morning!" we said back. We each began to go our own separate ways. I had a few deliveries to make, and Kris was making a phone call to one of our customers.

> **"Shannon said Jaime got arrested in China, but that she's okay."**

As Kelly passed by us in the opposite direction, he looked over his shoulder and said, "By the way, Shannon called before you two arrived."

Kris and I both stopped what we were doing and almost said at the same time, "How are they? What did they say?"

"Shannon said Jaime got arrested in China, but that she's okay," Kelly said.

"*What!*" Kris yelled out. He said that in that moment, all kinds of thoughts flooded his mind. With the questions in his brain swarming out of control, he tried to take charge of himself and let each question come out of his mouth one at a time. "Why was she arrested? What did she do?" he asked his brother.

"That's all I know," answered Kelly. "Shannon said that she'll call again in a few days.

"A few days! There's no way I can wait two more days to find out what's going on," Kris said as he left the room in frustration.

I was in shock. Our girls were in a foreign country seven thousand miles away from us. It was not as if I could hop in my car and drive cheerfully over to see them. We decided to be proactive and call several parents of the kids who were with our girls, to see if they had any more information. You have to remember, this happened in the early 1990s. People did not have cell phones back then, so it was much harder to get in touch with someone. We called around, to no avail. Everyone we tried to contact had not heard at all from their kids. Now it was a waiting game—only this game wasn't any fun, and I definitely didn't want to play!

Taking on the World

The next day, Jaime called us. "Thank God!" Kris said as he answered the phone. "Are you all right?" he asked.

"I'm fine, Dad. Really, I'm fine," Jaime said.

"What happened?" Kris asked.

Jaime began to tell us her story. Evidently, when her teammates were going through customs, she and one of her friends were pulled aside and questioned by the authorities. They found out that the two girls were carrying Bibles with them, and because of that, the girls were put into a small room with an officer who began interrogating them. I don't know if the officer didn't like the answers the girls were giving or what, but she turned more aggressive and began to pat down our daughter.

Frightened but praying all the while, Jaime did what she could to seem cooperative and urged her very upset friend to do the same. After about an hour had gone by, the officer finally let the two girls leave. Feeling the tension beginning to leave their bodies, they quickly exited customs to join the rest of their team. Here my daughter was, fourteen years old, and already she had her own international testimony to tell. She had learned that the power of God was on her life, and that when the Lord says He will be with us every step of the way, He means it.

"Were you scared?" I asked.

"Not too badly," Jaime said.

I love how resilient kids are. She didn't think it was a very big deal. At least, she didn't after it was all over with. Jaime just knew that she was on a mission, and she was prepared and ready to handle any obstacle that came her way.

Three days later, Kris and I were sound asleep when the phone began to ring. I looked at the clock, and it read 1:00 a.m. My heart began to pound. "Kris, Kris, wake up," I said. "The phone is ringing."

It is never good news when someone calls in the middle of the night. "Hello," Kris said.

"Daddy, Daddy!" said a sobbing Shannon. "I'm lost, and I don't know where I am!"

"Just take a breath, Shannon," Kris said. "Look around you. Do you recognize anything? Does anything look familiar to you?"

"No, Dad," Shannon said. "A few people stopped to help me, but nobody speaks English here. I called what would be equivalent to 911 in the States, and I've been looking for a policeman, but I haven't seen one," Shannon said between sobs.

"It's going to be all right," Kris said. "Let's pray."

Just as soon as Kris prayed for Shannon, a policeman showed up at the phone booth. The officer understood English and said he would arrange to take her back to the hotel where she was staying. At the same moment, the pastor of the church the team was ministering at just happened to see Shannon with the police officer. Pulling his van to the side, he explained to the officer that Shannon was with their church. Seeing that she was scared and anxious to leave, the driver scooped Shannon up and took her back to her hotel.

It was amazing to hear these stories from my girls' point of view. They loved every minute of their little adventure. In fact, we received one more phone call from them while they were on the mission trip. Each of them had the same request: "We want to stay in Hong Kong!"

You can imagine our response to that statement. As parents, we want to make sure our kids are well protected from anything that can harm them. Just look at how a mama animal rises up to protect her young. But at some point, we need to stretch out our kids' tent pegs a bit. The question here is, At what age does this happen? Only you as your child's parent can answer that question. Each child matures differently. Some are able to handle more responsibility at a younger age than others. My girls were both very mature and were making good decisions, showing Kris and me that they were able to take on more responsibility.

> **When the time is right, let your kids spread their wings and make some memories of their own.**

Do I recommend that our responses to our girls as they grew in age and maturity be superimposed over your family? Probably not. You know your children and what's best for them. Yet take the opportunities that come your way and make some great memories with your family. And when the time is right, let your kids spread their wings and make some memories of their own. Memories last a lifetime, and there is no time like the present to make them!

The Great Outdoors

Besides Kris, my son Jason has been my biggest encourager when it comes to adventure. Hunting and fishing are definitely in the Vallotton bloodline. From as far back as we know, the Vallotton clan fished and hunted daily. We have some family photos of Kris's grandpa with his boys. The boys were holding stringers of freshly caught fish, and the grins on their faces told it all.

Unfortunately, Kris did not inherit those genes from his father. Kris's dad died when he was three years old, leaving a void empty of any hunting or fishing experience in Kris's early years. Several years later, his mom married a man who was not a very good father. In the early years, his stepfather would not let Kris have any form of contact with his father's side of the family. Not only was Kris forbidden to have contact with his grandparents, but his stepfather never took an interest in Kris, either. It is so sad for someone to be so insecure that just because of jealousy, he or she would stand between a child and a family who loves that child. It is hard for me to understand this kind of behavior. Thankfully, a few years before his death, Kris's stepfather accepted the Lord into his life. God is such a redeemer!

Still, Kris tried to pass on a love of the great outdoors to our kids. When Jason was six years old, we bought him his first BB gun. He carried that thing around with him everywhere he went. Anything that moved was considered fair game in his eyes, which I am sure included our dog. We quickly realized that he needed a lesson in hunting etiquette: What you kill, you eat. Jason wore that gun out in two months! Before the summer was over, we replaced his gun two more times with a brand-new Daisy BB gun.

As Jay got a little older, we bought him a small compound bow. He was so proud of it and showed it off to everyone who showed any interest. I was not very good with a bow, but I would go outside with him and watch him practice behind our house. We had the perfect setup. With mostly forest behind us, all he needed were a few hay bales. Unfortunately, most of his arrows did not hit the bales. In fact, years later we were still finding arrows all over the woods behind our house. There were even a few strays that ended up high in the tree branches. But soon, Jay graduated on to bigger and better things.

> Years later we were still finding arrows all over the woods behind our house. There were even a few strays that ended up high in the tree branches.

When our boys, Gene and Jason, were in their teen years, hunting was still in their blood, especially Jason's. Again, I did not mind them shooting something, as long as they were going to eat it. We had two dogs at the time, each of them wanting to be right by the boys' side. The only problem was that the dogs messed up any chance of shooting anything. So when the two boys would go out on their way toward the woods, I would keep the dogs in the house. When dinnertime came around, I would tie a note on the collar of one of the dogs and let it loose. It never failed—the dogs always found the kids, no matter how far out they were from the house.

Once the dog with the note reached the boys, Jason would signal to me that they had been found by firing off a few rounds. The boys would come home with big smiles on their faces and show me their spoils. Then they would run to the dinner table. My biggest mistake was cleaning their catch instead of making them do it for themselves. They plopped whatever they had shot into my sink, knowing I would eventually come to their rescue and take care of it. Certainly, if I had it to do over again, that little detail would play out quite a bit differently.

Saddle Up!

Not everyone in the Vallotton home is adventurous in the same way. When my daughter Jaime went through a really "dark night of the soul," she began looking into ways to overcome her depression and anxiety. Someone had told her about equine therapy, and she started learning all she could about the benefits of working with horses. Jaime then bought a horse of her own, not really knowing what she was doing. Yet she felt it was what she needed to do. After a few months went by, Jaime proved a fast learner! Before I knew it, she was often up in the saddle. Clearly, she was longing for that deep connection with her horse that happens when you spend time together.

Jaime's horse was young, and Jaime was inexperienced. Together, they could have been a recipe for disaster. But Jaime was pushing past fear, stepping out of her prison of depression and totally submerging herself in her newfound passion. It was so beautiful to watch her from a distance. I began to feel a little jealous since I had always had a passion for horses, too. Watching her was bringing it all back.

Horseback riding was not completely foreign to me. I used to ride horses a bit when I was a kid. I even took my girls on a few trail rides when they were growing up. Jaime loved to ride, and the time she had spent on horseback was amazing, and still is. Shannon's riding experience had not been so wonderful. In fact, some of it was horrible. One time after Shannon had been married for a few years and was living in Etna, the three of us went riding. Three horses were stabled on the property she and her husband were renting, and the owners had said Shannon could use them to go riding anytime she wanted. We girls decided to enjoy the opportunity, but we didn't know much about any of the horses we were about to ride—mistake #1. Shannon's horse ended up being barn sour.

As the three of us took off on horseback down the road, everything started off amazing and we were enjoying the summer day. I felt as though I was riding off into the sunset, my head held high as the afternoon breeze gently whispered through my hair. It was so surreal. Nothing comes close to the peace you feel when you are out in the country, riding on the back of a horse as his steady gait lulls you down the path, as if there were not a care in the world. Still, we didn't want to take a long ride on our first outing and the temperature was rising, so we decided to turn around and head back to the barn.

Just as we were beginning to ride toward home, Shannon's horse took off in a full run, with Shannon screaming, face contorted, as she hung on for dear life.

> It is not as if riding horses is just a round of golf, especially when my first horse was only four years old when I bought him.

I galloped up beside her and grabbed the reins, pulling them to one side as I tried to stop her horse. Shannon had a look of terror written all over her face. I felt so bad! I wasn't scared at all; I was exhilarated! I could have ridden like that all day long. But I was 42 years old then. I am in my sixties now. Your age makes a big difference in your riding ability, especially when you haven't grown up in the saddle.

Years later, here I am today with three horses of my own, Dreamer, Legend and Bailey. I often ask myself, *What are you doing?* It is not as if riding horses is just a round of golf, especially when my first horse was only four years old when I bought him. I really had not been setting myself up to succeed at the time of the purchase, but I would not trade Dreamer for anything now. He still has a mind of his own, but now that he is older, he takes much better care of me than he did when he was younger. We are learning to trust one another in a healthy way. This does not just happen overnight. It takes lots of time and dedication. There have been good times and bad times. If only the two of us could both speak English, life would be so much simpler.

Bushwhacking Buddies

We have many trails throughout Shasta County that we are privileged to ride on. I try to take my horses riding off my property as much as possible. The change of scenery does us all good, and it is a great way to desensitize the horses to things they will encounter while being ridden. One time, my girlfriend Michelle and I decided to ride to a camp area called Horsetown. It's not a large area, but it has a nice creek that we love riding the horses through, especially on hot summer days.

We arrived at our favorite spot and let the horses play for a bit. They love splashing their hooves in the water, just as you would see a dog do. We had never explored much past the creek entrance and decided that this would be a great time to see what was lying ahead. Michelle was on my second horse, Legend, leading the way down a skinny path so lush green that it reminded me of a tropical forest. A few minutes into our ride, Legend stopped.

"What's up, Michelle?" I asked.

"There are quite a few low-lying vines in here, hanging from the tree branches," she answered, "but I think we can make it."

The vines were obscuring our path, but she thought she could move them to the side and still pass through. As she worked harder and harder on the vines, I could see that Legend was getting nervous. The vines were completely surrounding his head, and he was starting to panic.

"I think you need to get off Legend, Michelle," I said.

Dreamer was starting to react to Legend's fidgeting, and I felt as if this picture might turn ugly. As Michelle slipped down off Legend, the vines got twisted around the horn of his saddle. Legend pulled back, trying to free himself, and I heard a *snap* as he lunged backward and started running past me.

Before I could react, Dreamer was running after Legend, toward the main highway, taking me with him! My heart was racing as I tried to gather my thoughts. The path was a very narrow trail, mixed with boulders every few feet. Filled with twists and turns, it definitely was not conducive to anything faster than a walk.

Michelle began yelling at me, "Get off! Get off!"

I remember yelling back at her, "The only thing I can do now is ride this out!"

In case of an emergency, there is a maneuver called a "one-rein stop." By pulling on just one rein and bringing your horse's head around to the side, you can normally get it to stop. The only problem with this situation was that there was no safe place to try this move since Dreamer needed both his eyes on where he was stepping. If I had tried that move with him, he probably would have flipped, with me on him. And my vision wasn't great because my glasses had gone flying off my face when I had tried to duck under a low tree branch!

> I remember yelling back at her, "The only thing I can do now is ride this out!"

You are probably asking why I didn't just pull back on both reins and bring Dreamer to a stop. That might have worked if we had been by ourselves and Legend had not been racing away out in front of him. But horses are herd animals, and when they sense any kind of danger, they buddy up and run off together until they feel they are out of harm's way. Evidently, Legend didn't get the memo about being out of harm's way that day.

Michelle was still yelling as she took up the rear, "The highway, Kathy, the highway!"

I knew we were getting close to it, but I also remembered that there was an open meadow ahead with lots of green grass. "I'm sure he'll stop when he gets to the grass!" I yelled back.

Sure enough, Legend began to slow down to a trot in the meadow, and I was able to jump off Dreamer and grab Legend's reins. I didn't feel afraid until it was all over with. As soon as my heart stopped pounding in my chest, however, crazy thoughts began racing through my head. *What if Legend had not stopped and had run out onto the highway? What if Dreamer had followed and I had fallen?*

Finally, everything seemed to slow down to a standstill. Catching my breath, I thanked God for posting guardian angels along the path to protect us. Without God's protection, this could indeed have turned ugly. I have to say that this was the first and the last time we went bushwhacking through dense, low-lying strands of ivy. I definitely don't need a repeat of that adventure!

Life is too short not to do the things you love doing. The funny thing is, you might not even know that you love something if you don't try it. Fear keeps us from venturing out. It is the enemy's way of holding us in a state of entrapment.

> **Life is too short not to do the things you love doing. The funny thing is, you might not even know that you love something if you don't try it.**

Faith, on the other hand, is fear that has said its prayers. A great sense of accomplishment comes over us when we conquer our fears. With every victory, the enemy loses more and more of his grip, until all the threads that have entangled us are no longer wrapped around us, and we are free.

TWELVE

FOLLOWING BILL

*Where you go, I go; and where you live, I'll live. Your
people are my people, your God is my god.*

RUTH 1:16 MESSAGE

Bill and Beni Johnson left Weaverville in 1996 to become the senior leaders of Bethel Church in Redding, California, and Danny Silk became our new senior pastor at Mountain Chapel. We did not see the Johnsons much for a while since we were building our growing businesses, in the midst of raising a family of semi-adult kids who were quickly beginning to leave the nest. About a year later, Bill was traveling to Colorado to speak at a Youth With A Mission (YWAM) base where it happened that our daughter Jaime and her husband, Marty, were on staff. Bill asked Kris if he would like to come along with him to the base and catch up on life. Kris gladly accepted the offer, elated to be able to spend time with Bill again.

The week in Colorado was great for Kris. Not only did he get to see our kids and spend some time with Bill; he also was able to get away and have some God time. Our businesses were pretty all-consuming and, needless to say, very stressful. The break was a welcome relief for Kris, and I was really glad that he had decided to take that time off work, even if it meant I would need to pick up more responsibility in our Weaverville parts store. The week flew by, and Kris finally arrived home on the weekend. Little did I know that he was about to drop a huge bombshell in my lap.

"So tell me all about your week," were my opening words to Kris on his return. I was really excited to hear all the details. If you asked Kris, he would say that details are my love language. I wanted to hear every detail that I could.

Little did I know that he was about to drop a huge bombshell in my lap.

"The kids are doing great," he said. "They seem to be adjusting to married life and are settling down in their new surroundings. And Colorado is beautiful!"

"How was your time with Bill?" I asked. "I know you were really looking forward to being with him."

"It was great," Kris said. "God's favor is on his life so much, and I continually learn so much every time I'm with him."

"Did you talk about anything interesting?" I asked. At this point, I felt as though Kris was not releasing all the details, and this girl needed some!

Kris fed me a few more little details before he finally blurted out, "I'm in love with a man!" Then he spontaneously burst into tears.

"What do you mean?" I inquired.

Kris went on to tell me that he and Bill had stayed together in a small cabin for five days. Kris recounted how he passed by Bill's bunk bed to go to the restroom in the middle of the night, and Bill would be loving on Jesus in his sleep!

"Bill was saying, '*Jesus, I love You; Jesus, You are amazing*,' all night long! I was so taken aback by Bill's relationship with the Lord—not to mention seeing the impact Jesus has on Bill's spirit. It wrecked me!" Kris continued. "The Lord showed me that we're supposed to be with Bill for life! On the way home, we flew into San Francisco and had a layover there for a couple of hours. At lunch, Bill asked me if we would come and start a 'school of the prophets.'"

"Weaverville could really benefit from a school like that," I responded.

"Well, no, not Weaverville," Kris clarified. "Redding! He wants us to leave our businesses and move to Redding to start a full-time ministry school at Bethel," he explained.

When Reality Hits

When it hit me what Kris was actually saying, I couldn't believe what I was hearing. Never ever had I thought of us moving away from Weaverville. I cried. I cried a lot. I felt as though my heart and soul were being ripped apart. My life was never going to be the same. I didn't want my life to change—ever! But with the kids leaving the nest, it was happening right before my eyes. I felt as if my world was caving in around me. The dust was flying, and I couldn't breathe.

Kris was so positive that he had heard God speak to him about moving. God always speaks to him; I didn't question that. I just needed to hear the Lord speak to me personally about it. One evening, Kris and I were talking about what this potential move would look like. At the time, we had three parts stores in three different locations, along with an automotive air-conditioning remanufacturing business. We were insanely busy!

"What about all these businesses? What's going to happen to them?" I asked.

"We have managers who will continue to run them while we're in Redding, and the stores will provide a great retirement for us," Kris explained. "Or we'll sell them."

"I need to get out of here," I said to Kris in reply. I needed to try to hear from God myself. "There's a worship and prophetic conference next month at MorningStar, and I think I'm going to take the week and just get away."

Did I just say that? I wondered. I was always very quiet and reserved, but desperate times call for desperate measures. Within a few weeks, I was on a plane without my husband, headed to Fort Mill, South Carolina. This would be a new venture for me, one I would never forget.

I took Sarah, a friend of my two daughters, with me to South Carolina. Sarah loved MorningStar and wanted to take the opportunity to visit there with someone she knew. The plane ride was great. Sarah and I exchanged small talk as we dialogued back and forth about what we thought we might experience. When we finally arrived, Tracy Evans was waiting for us at the airport, ready to attend the conference with us.

The conference was wonderful. I loved worship leaders Don Potter and Suzy Wills. Their music was such a great expression of their love for God. They seemed to write their lyrics from their heart, from their most intimate experiences with God. That's what I needed—one of those intimate experiences with God.

Each night after the evening session was over, I would call home. Kris wanted to know all the details of my time at the conference. His last question would always be, "Well, did you hear from God yet?"

Each night, my response to his question would be "No." I was beginning to think that something was wrong with me. *I must not have a relationship with Jesus like Kris has*, I thought. *He's always hearing God's voice. But for me, not so much.*

Friday night came, the very last night of the conference. To be honest, I was disappointed and really just wanted to go home by then. I probably would have left if Tracy had not been with us. Worship was great, and the speaker for the night was Ray Hughes. I had heard about him, but I had never met him in person. He was a prophetic guy with a very heavy Southern accent. Worship ended, and Ray began speaking. He led with a few stories that made me laugh out loud; the guy was a comedian. But I was not at the conference to be entertained. I needed a word from God, and it sure didn't seem as if I would get it from this guy.

After about thirty minutes, Ray closed his notebook and said, "I don't know why I'm speaking from these notes. I feel as though God is giving me a fresh word." Then he started talking about people leaving the mountains and going to Bethlehem. Now, that got my attention! I honestly didn't remember much after that. Kris and I were obviously living in the mountains, and Bill was asking us to leave everything behind and come to Bethel.

I knelt down on the ground, tears streaming from my eyes, trying to make sense out of what had just happened to me.

The rest of what Ray said was a very prophetic blur. I knelt down on the ground, tears streaming from my eyes, trying to make sense out of what had just happened to me. It was as if Ray had disappeared and Jesus was standing right in front of my face. The Lord began to share all these things with me, and how He wanted Kris and me to be part of them. It seemed so overwhelming! I had never had an experience like that in my entire life.

I stood up and looked over at Tracy, who was as messed up as I was. We were having similar experiences. Just as we were leaving, a lady who was sitting behind me reached over and touched my shoulder. She said, "Don't be surprised if what you heard wasn't what he said."

Now, that was a weird statement, I thought, *but hey, this is a prophetic conference.* Afterward, Tracy and I exchanged stories about our experiences in that session. Eager to listen to what Ray had actually said, I purchased the session's audiotape. Tracy and I found a cassette recorder and popped in the tape. Ray's fresh word was not there! The recording stopped short of it, and it had not been recorded.

We couldn't believe it. "I'm sure the session was video-recorded. Let's just purchase the VHS tape," I suggested. I bought the tape, anxious to watch it.

Then Tracy looked at me with a crooked smile on her face. "I don't have a VHS player," she said.

"That's okay, we have one at home. I'll watch it there," I said. Meanwhile, I couldn't wait to call Kris. The phone rang a few times, and finally he picked up.

"I heard from God! I heard from God!" I nearly shouted into the phone.

I must have been rambling, because Kris finally blurted out, "Slow down! I can't understand what you're saying."

I began to catch my breath and repeat everything that the Lord had shown me, trying not to leave anything out. "I have a VHS tape, and I pray it's all on there," I told Kris. "I can't wait until you hear the word Ray spoke. I have to go pack now. I'll see you tomorrow!"

The next day, Kris picked me up from the airport and took me right home. I don't know who was more excited, him or me. We walked into the house, and the first thing I did was pop the tape into the player. Fast-forwarding to the exact spot where Ray closed his notes and started giving the word, I pressed *Play*.

"Here it is! Here it is!" I said. We listened intently to every word Ray spoke. He talked about the mountains and Bethlehem, but the rest was not anything like I remembered hearing. I rewound the tape. Then I fast-forwarded the tape. I sat there puzzled about what I was seeing and hearing.

"Is this what you were looking for?" Kris asked. "This isn't anything like what you told me."

"Honestly, honey, I'm not sure about anything now. I'm so confused," I murmured.

Just then, I remembered what the lady behind me had said: *"Don't be surprised if what you heard is not what he said."*

In the moment I had thought her statement was really weird, but that must have been it. God was using a guy I didn't even know to get my attention, and in an instant my world was changed. I experienced a touch from God that went far beyond my mind or intellect. It pierced my spirit in such a way that I was marked for the rest of my life.

Scared to Live

Hearing the truth is one thing, but believing it is another. Even after experiencing such a wonderful touch from God, I spent days behaving like my corralled horses when they had been surrounded by a strand of electric fencing wire for the first time. They had refused to exit through the corral gate, fearing that they would be shocked as they passed through to the other side. I tried everything I could think of to coax them through the gate, but nothing worked. I finally dispelled their anxiety by walking back and forth through the gate while they looked on. It took about ten minutes of showing them that they had nothing to fear before they reluctantly ran through the gate.

> We cannot let our past circumstances redefine our present reality and reduce our God-given destiny to what we feel we can handle.

Through the experience I had with my horses, I learned that God always opens a gate to our promises, but we must trust Him to lead us into painless pastures. We cannot let our past circumstances redefine our present reality and reduce our God-given destiny to what we feel we can handle. Now the true test for me was about to happen.

After much prayer and dialogue, Kris and I decided that the best plan for our future was to sell the businesses so we could give our whole heart to Bill and Bethel. I guess Kris was finally getting his prayer answered after twenty years: *I don't want to be in business. I want to be in the ministry!*

We met with the Big A executives and told them we were going to sell our stores and go into full-time ministry. They immediately offered to buy all three of our stores. We opened an escrow account and began the process. This business transaction was only supposed to take ninety days, but we kept running into unforeseen delays on their end. Soon, eighteen months had passed. We did not think much of it because the company kept auditing our books every three to six months and assuring us that things were moving along just fine. In the middle of all this, we moved to Redding and began building the ministry school while our managers ran the auto parts stores.

Then came that terrifying Monday morning when one of our managers called the Big A warehouse for a special-order part. Instead of the warehouse answering the call, our manager got a recording that said, "I'm sorry, but you have reached a number that has been disconnected or is no longer in service."

What the heck? We called our rep, and his number had also been disconnected. Soon, other auto part stores were calling us to see if we knew anything.

"This is crazy!" we contended. The final blow came when we opened up a certified letter that was hand-delivered to us. It informed us that Big A had just filed for bankruptcy. Talk about a shock! I didn't know what to think. The scary thing about it was that we owed well over 1.8 million dollars to suppliers all over the country. This debt was part of our purchase agreement with Big A and was to be paid off in the escrow, along with about $250,000 coming to us personally. But now we were sinking so deep that no one could pull us out.

Fight or Quit

How could God let this happen to us? We had always tried to do everything He asked of us. We just couldn't believe it. There was frantic tension all around. I was losing my peace and desperately needed to find it. Then the biggest of all blows came about three days later. The bankruptcy court was calling our note due and giving us thirty days to pay the debt in full. This was the final straw.

What do you do in a situation like this? When things are crumbling all around you, just remember that Jesus is in the middle of your storm. You are not alone. He says that He will never leave us or forsake us. What a promise, and the great news is that He is a promise keeper. He does not lie or fail to come through on His Word. I love the fact that He can see all the way to the end, and He knows the best path for each of us to take. I should never try to second-guess Him. He is the One who is all knowing, and He knows what is best for my family. He knows what I can handle and what I cannot. My welfare and the welfare of my family are always in the forefront of His mind. Jesus knows what it will take to shape me and mold me into the best me I can be.

Although I knew all of this and thought I believed it, I was really struggling. By the time we received the letter from the bankruptcy court, Kris and I were living in a small apartment in Redding, which was about all we could afford. Neither Kris nor I was getting paid from Bethel. We had just launched Bethel School of Supernatural Ministry, and things were really tight. Both of us had agreed to work for free the first year, knowing that the next year we would both get paid. We came prepared for this when we accepted the job. Our main financial support was supposed to come from our business sale, not from Bethel.

Where was the peace I once had felt? I didn't want to continue on like this anymore. Every day, I woke up feeling as if there were another nail being pounded deep into my heart. I remember telling the Lord that I knew we had been launched into business by a prophetic word, but I felt as if the season had changed and we somehow had missed the turn.

I felt as if the season had changed and we somehow had missed the turn.

Kris was also weary, but he was ready to fight back. The guy never gives up! He wanted to step back into the stores and rebuild our company. He was trying to inspire me to courage. But I was at my wits' end, and one morning I rolled over in bed, looked Kris in the eyes and said something I have never said to him before: "I'm not doing this anymore!"

"What aren't you doing?" he asked.

"Business. I'm done. This needs to end today!"

I know Kris felt as though I had just stabbed him in the heart and shattered his dream. It ripped my guts out to tell him I was done, especially since we had invested everything that we had into our business. For years, many times I would hold things inside me, not wanting to disappoint my husband. But this time, I felt as though God had given me the strength to speak up.

After a few moments of silence, Kris got out of bed, picked up the phone and called our bank. With tears rolling down his face, Kris began telling our bank manager (who was also our friend) that we could not continue on in our business anymore and that we appreciated all the grace and mercy he had extended to us over the years. He went on to tell him that he would be in later on in the day to turn our keys over to him. He hung up the phone and cried for hours. The warrior had faced a major defeat, and he was brokenhearted and ashamed.

Despite everything we were feeling, the decision to leave business behind us brought a sense of closure. There was peace in the air again, and I knew we could face anything that would be coming our way due to the repercussions of our decision. The ton of bricks I had been carrying on my shoulders for months had just become a whole lot lighter. I felt sure that we were poised for another miracle.

Beauty from Ashes

I also knew it was time for me . . . for us . . . to dream again. I had to come to grips with the reality that our "little house on the prairie" season was over. Our dream house in the woods had been lost in our business venture gone bad. Life would never be the same again. Then I started thinking about the question my friend had asked me many years earlier: "What do you dream about, Kathy?" I have to admit that I was gun-shy. It was hard to get my hopes up enough to dream again, especially after all we had been through. Yet something crazy happened. We somehow entered a miracle vortex much like the one we had been in during the beginning years of owning the 76 station. Literally miracle after miracle started happening all around us. First, our main supplier, Big A, forgave us around $900,000 of the debt we owed. That alone was incredible, and I remember being so thankful for all the miraculous reductions. But there was still so much more to pay.

> **We somehow entered a miracle vortex. . . . Literally miracle after miracle started happening all around us.**

We still owed another major debt of around $300,000 on a Small Business Administration (SBA) loan. A representative from the SBA came by to speak with us. "You realize how much money you owe us?" this rep said.

"Yes, we are well aware of our debt. However, we have no money at this time to pay you," Kris countered.

"Make us an offer you can afford, then," the SBA rep told us, like extending an offer in compromise.

"Look, I don't mean to be rude, but we don't even know how we're going to pay our rent this month," Kris responded.

The rep stared at Kris with a serious look and said, "Kris, please just give me an amount that I can write down on this form so I can hand this offer over to my boss. What about $10,000?"

Kris and I both laughed, and Kris confessed, "Offering to pay $10,000 on a $300,000 note? What an insult that would be to the bank. But okay, if you say so, $10,000 it is."

Of course, neither one of us had any idea where we would get $10,000. The fact is, people were bringing us groceries by that time. Still, we signed an official document offering $10,000 to the SBA, and the representative left.

Several days later, we got a call. "Kris and Kathy," the rep said, "the SBA didn't accept your offer."

That was no surprise to either one of us. "Thank you for trying," we said.

"Hold on!" the rep said. "They made you a counteroffer."

"Okay, how much would they accept?"

"We won't accept the $10,000 offer, but we will accept $11,000," the rep proclaimed.

"$11,000!" we shouted.

"But there is a stipulation: You have only thirty days to pay it off, or the deal is off the table."

Twenty-eight long days passed with no activity, but God wasn't finished with us yet. On the twenty-ninth day of our SBA deadline, a person we didn't know gave Kris a check for $30,000! Not only could we pay off the $11,000 to the SBA; the gift also allowed us to pay off the California State Board of Equalization, along with paying the IRS for payroll taxes we owed.

As a little side note, when we called the SBA representative to say we were bringing the check to the SBA office, the rep cried and told us about praying for us throughout this time. Over the next three years, all of our more than $1.8-million debt was paid off or forgiven, without us ever filing for bankruptcy.

Dreams Really Do Come True

The truth is that I was actually afraid to dream again, not because dreaming is risky, which of course it is, but because I didn't think I deserved anything more. How many times did the Lord have to bail us out? God had already given us more than our share. *A person shouldn't be greedy*, I reasoned. Redding really was a great place to live, despite the very hot summers. There was always something to do for recreation, and stores stayed open past sundown, unlike Weaverville. I was happy and content with my life just the way it was; I really didn't need anything else.

But then the Lord began to talk to me: *Not everything is about money or possessions. What about love, influence, supporting others or making a difference in someone's life? It's not what you can get that makes a difference, but what you can give and do for others. That's what changes lives!*

> "It's not what you can get that makes a difference, but what you can give and do for others. That's what changes lives!"

Forty-five years have passed since I married the man of my dreams and we set out on this journey to follow God at any cost. I realize as I sit here writing this book that many people dream only of their desired positions or wanted possessions. I, on the other hand, have been dreaming all my life of serving others. I get completely energized every time there is an opportunity that comes my way to serve people, especially those who have loved me and looked out for my best interest.

God has blessed me with many people in my life, but there is one in particular who stands out above the rest. That one is Kris! He is my hero. He has always been there, encouraging me in everything I do. I may not have faith in my abilities, but he sure does. My husband is one of the most giving men I have ever met. His life, his dreams and his desires have been laid down for the sake of others over and over again. Kris's life is a true picture of Jesus' hand extended, and I get to take part in sharing that love. He has been a great role model for me to follow. My deepest desire and my greatest dream is that Kris would become all God has called him to be. He thrives in tough times. Kris has an amazing ability to walk into a bad situation and know exactly what to do to make something right again.

My husband is an executor, one who is a dreamer and a visionary. I am one who does not like the spotlight. I love being in the background and helping him thrive, however. I love taking on his dream and making it come true. I love to create, whether it is with music, building something with my hands or creating something with words. Kris and I are the perfect team. I could not even think of doing life without him.

After all these years, I have learned a few things about life, love and dreaming. I have learned that dreams really do come true—at least "God dreams" do—but often not in the way we think they will, and not on our timeline. I have also learned that dreams of positions and possessions are often God's way of luring us into identity, purpose and character, while drawing us into a deeper level of trust in Him.

I know now that the only real "little house on the prairie" fulfillment of my dreams lies in the heart of our heavenly Father. People can take away our house, our land, our position and our possessions, but they cannot rob us of the true treasure we gain being on our journey of life in Jesus.

THIRTEEN

QUESTION REALITY

*So, as those who have been chosen of God, holy and beloved,
put on a heart of compassion, kindness, humility, gentleness
and patience; bearing with one another, and forgiving each
other, whoever has a complaint against anyone; just as
the Lord forgave you, so also should you. Beyond all these
things put on love, which is the perfect bond of unity.*

COLOSSIANS 3:12–14

I can't believe that he could be so rude! I said to myself. The
thoughts I had going through my mind were incredibly painful.

I had been part of the worship team at Bethel for years. I led
worship on the weekends and also played the keyboard and the violin.
On this particular evening, I was playing my violin during a conference
where Brian Johnson was leading with his guitar. The atmosphere was
heavy with the presence of God. People were engaged in worship, taken

in by God's beauty and the weightiness of His presence. It was one of those moments that felt as if heaven was within reach.

As Brian began to take us deeper into God's presence, the worship created a moment that literally yearned for the violin and cello. Stringed instruments have such a prophetic voice that fits beautifully into these epic expressions of worship. My friend Michelle and I began to play as the congregation gave themselves to ministering to the Lord. While we were playing, I thought I saw something out of the corner of my eye. It looked as if Brian were motioning to us to play something different, but I couldn't quite figure out what he was trying to say. I stared at him for several minutes, to try to get some clarity, while growing more nervous by the minute. The worship teams have used hand signals for years to communicate with each other during live worship sets. Those signals are easy to miss if you are not paying attention, which can be quite frustrating for the band leader.

I continued to watch Brian intently as we played, still trying to discern what he was trying to communicate to us. Suddenly, he took his hand away from his guitar and began to swing it back toward us, as if to shush us up from playing. I have to tell you, that felt really rude! I figured he could have put his hand behind his back and just signaled to us to stop playing, but instead, his motions made it look as if he were upset with us. He was abruptly flicking his hand from side to side, directing it right at us.

Michelle and I stared at each other in total confusion. I knew then that what I saw Brian doing was not a figment of my imagination. Michelle and I didn't exchange any words, but I could tell she was having the same struggle as I was, so we both just stopped playing.

I can't believe him. What does he think he's doing? I thought. We waited until the next song started and began to play out softly at the appropriate moment. It felt as if everything was back to normal. Brian seemed happy, and Michelle had relaxed once again. All of a sudden,

Brian started swinging his hand around again in a violent expression of what I thought was frustration.

I can't even begin to tell you what was running through my mind. I remember thinking, *That's it! I'm not doing this anymore. I've been like a mother to Brian. I took care of him when he was a baby. I changed his dirty diapers and wiped his snotty nose. He was over to our house all the time and has always been like one of our family.* I wrestled with my thoughts. *Why couldn't he just have motioned for us to stop playing? Why did he have to humiliate us in front of everyone?*

> I knew that God was trying to engage me, and suddenly I found myself arguing with Him. Worse yet, I was losing.

I knew everyone had seen what was going on, and it sure was embarrassing. *No problem,* I thought. *This is the last time I am ever going to play for this team. I don't have to put up with this anymore,* I fumed inwardly, resolving to resign from the team on Monday.

What are you doing? asked a still, small voice in my head.

I knew that God was trying to engage me, and suddenly I found myself arguing with Him. Worse yet, I was losing.

You aren't doing anything until you talk to Brian, God demanded of me.

No way! I fought back. *I'm done.*

You are a coward! the Lord insisted.

No, I'm not!

Yes, you are. You call yourself a leader, but you refuse to confront Brian, the Lord continued.

Ugh! I knew that God wouldn't stop until I agreed to talk with Brian. *Okay, okay,* I said, *I'll talk to him.*

Worship ended, and we got ready to exit the stage. I stalled a bit, hoping that Brian had already left. I looked up and he was still onstage, fiddling with his guitar. *Darn! The Lord isn't making this easy for me*, I mused, *but I just want it to be over with. Here goes!* As I walked toward him, Brian glanced up and looked right at me.

"Hey, Brian, what was that all about back there?" I asked.

"What do you mean?" he questioned.

"You know what I'm talking about," I blurted out.

"I have no idea what you mean," Brian said in a confused tone.

"Brian! During worship you began to swing your hand in a really angry fashion, telling Michelle and me to stop playing."

"No, I didn't!" exclaimed Brian.

"Everyone saw you!" I said in a combative tone.

This was probably a bit of an exaggeration on my part, but in the moment, it sure felt true to me. I recounted everything that had gone on in my head during worship, followed by how humiliated Michelle and I had felt by his actions.

"Oh, I know!" He burst out in laughter.

He's laughing . . . really? Could this get any worse? I thought.

"While I was playing, a fly started buzzing around my face," Brian explained. "It was driving me crazy! I must have been swinging my arm around, trying to get it away from my face," he said, still laughing.

A fly buzzing around his face! I chided myself. *I can't believe I allowed myself to have so many terrible thoughts about Brian over a fly.*

"I am so sorry about this!" I said. We both looked at each other and began to laugh as we finished packing up our instruments and got ready to leave the sanctuary.

Feeding the Enemy's Thoughts

I can't tell you how foolish I felt, but the worst part of it all was the fact that I had allowed my thoughts to travel so far down the path of destruction. Thankfully, Brian thought it was funny.

Isn't it just like the enemy of our souls to seed our minds with destructive thoughts and fertilize them with some manure? Then we come along and water them like there is no tomorrow. What was a passing thought in my mind had turned into the creature from the black lagoon, slime and all. I should have known better than to play into the ploys of the devil.

The apostle Paul warned us about this demonic dynamic. He wrote, "We are destroying speculations and every lofty thing raised up against the knowledge of God, and we are taking every thought captive to the obedience of Christ" (2 Corinthians 10:5).

For instance, your daughter is late coming home from school and you suddenly think, *What if someone kidnapped her?* Have you ever noticed that the what-ifs in our minds are nearly always negative? When was the last time you thought something positive as a what-if? *Maybe the school principal took my daughter aside and gave her the Outstanding Achievement award!* But no . . . it's always something horrible that our minds gravitate toward.

Do you know what a "lofty thing" is? It is an idea that is bigger than God.

"What? Nothing is bigger than God!" you protest. Technically, that's true, but whenever we worry, we have fallen for the lie that our problem is beyond either God's care for us or His ability to solve our issue. Worry is actually irrational if we know who we are and whose we are.

> **Whenever we worry, we have fallen for the lie that our problem is beyond either God's care for us or His ability to solve our issue. Worry is actually irrational if we know who we are and whose we are.**

Then there are those plaguing thoughts that run through our minds like a bad song we just cannot seem to ditch. I like the way Kris describes these destructive ideas by telling the story of a gal whom he saw walking a couple of dogs. She was a small lady who was taking her two huge 150-pound dogs for a walk. They were dragging her down the street, pooping on people's lawns and peeing on their bushes, while she tried her best to yank them back into the street. Our thoughts are often like those unruly dogs, dragging our minds from tormenting thought to tormenting thought. Instead of us telling our minds what to think, our minds dictate our thinking narrative, while we attempt to keep the "dogs" busy by feeding them some treats. Yet the apostle Paul instructs us to be "taking every thought captive." In other words, bad thoughts ought to become our POWs. We ought not allow them to run free or drag us along like a Jet Ski in a cesspool. Taking every thought captive is obedience training for our minds.

My life verses, which I already quoted once and probably will again because they are so important to me, deal with this very issue:

Finally, brethren, whatever is true, whatever is honorable, whatever is right, whatever is pure, whatever is lovely, whatever is of good repute, if there is any excellence and if anything worthy of praise, dwell on these things. The things you have learned and received and heard and seen in me, practice these things, and the God of peace will be with you.

Philippians 4:8–9

When we feast our minds on the Word of God, digest the testimonies of Jesus and meditate on the Holy Spirit's prophetic declarations over our lives, we break the cycle of negative thinking, and we rest in God's peace.

I should have followed the apostle Paul's instructions with Brian, because I know that Brian loves me and would not do something on purpose to embarrass me in front of hundreds of people. I should have realized that there was another reason or explanation for what I was seeing. But instead of acting in a reasonable manner, I acted like the lady with the big dogs. I reacted to the experience and created a monster in my mind. I even went so far as to feed the monster, not stopping to think about the destruction I was doing to myself—not to mention to my relationship with Brian.

Confrontation Forges Character

Trust is the train track of relationships, and communication is the train. That being said, it is crazy to me that our children go to school to learn math, reading and writing, and they also study history and science, yet they are seldom taught how to actually communicate with other human beings. Consequently, many of them (and many of us) struggle in this area. We are often at a real disadvantage in relationships.

Communication is more than forming words with our mouths or making intelligent sounds. Communication is an art that we must master if we are going to accomplish anything profound in life. Furthermore, there are many forms of communication, but the one I have struggled with the most is confrontation. Confrontation has gained a negative connotation over the years. Before coming to Bethel, I would rather have done anything besides confront someone. That is because confrontation rarely goes well for those of us who fear it, usually because we don't confront a person until our anger overcomes our fear. Of course, by then we are not trying to reconcile with the person; instead, we are out for justice.

> Sometimes encouraging people toward the best God has for them might involve confrontation.

Thankfully, that has changed for me since I have been on staff at Bethel. I have come to realize that if God loves us too much to leave us the way we are, then shouldn't we also want the very best for the people He has placed in our lives? Sometimes encouraging people toward the best

God has for them might involve confrontation. We cannot let our fear of confrontation dictate other people's future.

Whenever we interact with others in a way that involves confrontation, however, it should always be from a place of love. If confrontation feels like vengeance, then we are not responding from a place of love. The Bible says love "bears all things, believes all things, hopes all things, endures all things" (1 Corinthians 13:7). When we confront people, we therefore cannot expect instant results, since transformation and change often take time.

People are complex creatures, and there are often many layers to their issues and situations. Getting to the truth and forcing lies to the surface so they can be uprooted is sometimes a complicated journey. This process reminds me, metaphorically speaking, of a project Kris and I took on one winter. Our grandkids were all very young, and we thought it would be awesome to make each family their own toy box for Christmas. Kris has done a lot of woodwork over the years; he even built me a cedar hope chest in high school. Yet I wanted the toy boxes to be from both of us, so I was determined to contribute to the project in whatever way Kris thought I could.

The first order of business was for me to familiarize myself with each piece of equipment we were using. Next, the two of us organized the wood to make sure we had enough to complete all four boxes. Then Kris began to run each board through a machine called a planer that milled each board to the correct thickness. After that step was complete, Kris began joining three boards together for the top of the box, as well as joining the four sides. Meanwhile, I was tasked with using a sander to make every piece of wood smooth to the touch.

"Go ahead and work on sanding each section, and I'll come back and check on your work," Kris instructed.

This will be easy, I thought to myself. *I can't mess this up too badly.* Soon I announced to Kris, "I'm all done."

Kris came over to check on my progress. "No, you're not," he pushed back.

"Feel the boards," I said.

"I know they look smooth, but wait until we treat the wood," Kris said. He began to paint some sort of solution over every square inch of the wood. "Wait about ten minutes for this process to be complete," he insisted.

I was a bit frustrated, because to me the wood looked perfectly smooth and I was ready to move on to the next step.

"Okay," Kris soon said, "now that the wood is dry, rub your hand over the top of the boards."

I couldn't believe how rough it felt. "Where did that come from?" I asked.

"The grain will continue to rise until it has been completely sanded away. It's a process you're going to have to repeat three more times. Each time you repeat the process, you need to re-sand the boards before applying the solution again. This will ensure that when we apply the final finish, all of the grain will remain smooth. Once this process is complete, we can move on to the next step," he said.

I had a revelation while I was working on the kids' toy box projects. I imagined people as those toy chests, and I imagined the raised grain as the rough parts of our character that God is sanding smooth with the sander called life. I thought about how often we avoid the uncomfortable "sanding" process of our journey and settle for having rough rather than noble character. We refuse to face the truth and instead look for painless, symptomatic cures to our character issues, but this doesn't bring real restoration to our souls. Then these wounds fester beneath the surface

> **The best thing we can do for ourselves and for those we love is to learn the art of the give-and-take of honest communication.**

of our innermost being and are often exposed at the most inopportune time.

The best thing we can do for ourselves and for those we love is to learn the art of the give-and-take of honest communication. It is in the "iron sharpening iron" process that great character is forged. Kris is such a good example in my life of loving people well in this way. He is proficient with the "sander" of confrontation. His ability to see a problem and address a solution, while at the same time bringing hope to everyone he works with, is one of his greatest assets. He is a man who is not afraid to confront people when needed, yet he walks in such humility and grace. I think the reason he excels in this area is because he loves people well and actually wants the very best for others. This is my man, the one whom I chose to do life with. I wouldn't have it any other way.

FOURTEEN

THE ME
I HARDLY KNOW

Now the word of the LORD came to me saying,
"Before I formed you in the womb I knew you, and
before you were born I consecrated you."

JEREMIAH 1:4–5

Kris and I were speaking at a church in Texas several years ago. The service began, and we entered into a really deep place in worship. We were singing about the beauty of God, and I found myself captivated . . . lost in the song's words of adoration for the Father. As the song was coming to an end, I heard the Lord say, *Ask Me what I think is beautiful.*

Okay, God, what do You think is beautiful? I responded.

I felt Him put His arms around me and say, *You are. And I want you to "be you, till you're full" of everything that I have placed inside you!*

Wow, I was completely undone! I felt as though the Lord was shaking me, and everything that was not "me" was falling off, while everything holy and authentic remained. From that day on, I saw myself so much more clearly through the eyes of Jesus.

It's funny, because when I was a child, I used to play dress-up and have tea parties with my stuffed animals in my room. Nothing was real, just a fantasy in my mind that served as entertainment for a short while. I could become anyone I wanted to be. Reality didn't matter, because I was alive in my imagination. In those early years of my childhood, I would often wander off into never-never land and not have a care in the world. Other times, I would fly away to some famous place and perform on the greatest stages in America, all in the name of being "someone else."

Then one day, after the Lord told me I was beautiful to Him, I was pondering what He had said to me. In that moment, I realized that in a way, I had never really grown up. I still often imagined myself being somebody else. I came to understand that I was uncomfortable with my weaknesses, and that I didn't actually like a lot of things about myself. So I kept imagining being someone else. But the Lord was wooing me into womanhood and challenging me to be authentic and real. His description of my beauty was to *"be you, till you're full"* of everything that *I have placed inside you!*

I could see for the first time that my efforts to be someone else were keeping me from being an original of myself.

Thinking about all of this, I could see for the first time that my efforts to be someone else were keeping me from being an original of myself. I thought about my children and how each one of them is so different from the others, yet it is their unique qualities that I love the most about them. As a mom, I celebrate their distinct personalities and even their quirky traits. I am careful not to compare my children with each other or pressure them to conform. After all, if we pressure our children into becoming clones of someone else, they will never discover the history-making role God has assigned to them alone.

Who Does God Say I Am?

I knew it was time for me to stop pretending to be someone else, and to learn to love the person I was created to be. This was a challenge, because I was unsure of who I was. I sat down at my computer and began to write down what God said about me. I felt a bit sheepish at first, writing down my strengths, and I was scared even to look at my weaknesses.

In the midst of my journey toward authenticity, I began pondering the word *weakness*, and I remembered what the great apostle Paul had written about his own life: "Therefore I take pleasure in infirmities, in reproaches, in needs, in persecutions, in distresses, for Christ's sake. For when I am weak, then I am strong" (2 Corinthians 12:10 NKJV). Gradually, I came to understand that it is in my weakness that I am made strong. Furthermore, it is my weakness that gives me the opportunity to experience God's strength and learn to trust Him instead of myself.

The truth is, I have always thought of myself as a strong woman, physically, mentally and spiritually. There are not many things in life that really rattle my soul, and I have been able to glide through most of life's situations with a high level of peace. At least, that's what I have told myself. Yet recently, I have become aware that something has changed in me as I have gotten older. I noticed that I am not as much of a risk taker as I was in my youth. As I mentioned earlier, I have never rivaled Kris in taking risks; he has always been the daring one. But over time, I seemed to become a lot less daring than I used to be. I wanted to believe that I simply was becoming increasingly careful because of the great wisdom and maturity I have accumulated over the years. That sounds so spiritual, right? Little did I realize that God was about to unearth the bars of my prison and invite me to live in true freedom.

Virus Fear

It all started in late 2019, when China broke out with a virus that would shut down their entire country. By the spring of 2020, COVID-19, or the coronavirus, spanned the globe. It affected everyone somehow, and no one was spared. In the first few days of the pandemic, people were unsure what to expect. But soon our government was telling us what we could and could not do. One of the first decrees was that our gatherings could not exceed 250 people. By the end of the week, that number was downsized to 50, and the very next day, the number was lowered to 10 or fewer people in a room.

Deep uncertainty filled our nation as anxiety seeped into the hearts and minds of the people in our communities. Stores and businesses were ordered to close, and day after painful day, we watched our freedoms slip away. A spirit of fear ran roughshod over us as millions of people started hoarding food and supplies, especially toilet paper.

In the midst of my inner war, I remembered what King Solomon wrote: "The name of the LORD is a strong tower; the righteous runs into it and is safe" (Proverbs 18:10).

Despite my history of living a life of peace, I, too, found myself victimized by this evil spirit. I was giving in to its grasp and being sucked into the undertow of its current. Kris kept asking me how I was doing (I think he could sense my unrest), and every day I would tell him I was doing fine. But in reality, that was not the truth. My mind was in an intense battle to find peace as the enemy chucked terrifying thoughts into my fortress like grenades thrown on a battlefield. I often found myself ducking for cover and longing for solace. The trial was kicking my butt, and God was exposing my weakness.

In the midst of my inner war, I remembered what King Solomon wrote: "The name of the LORD is a strong tower; the righteous runs into it and is safe" (Proverbs 18:10). I felt God summoning me into His tower, and I had a deep conviction that He wanted to wash away my fears with His Word. I picked up the Message Bible and turned to my favorite passage, which you can probably guess since I've already quoted it twice. I began reading it out loud to myself:

Summing it all up, friends, I'd say you'll do best by filling your minds and meditating on things true, noble, reputable, authentic, compelling, gracious—the best, not the worst; the beautiful, not the ugly; things to praise, not things to curse. Put into practice what you learned from me, what you heard and saw and realized. Do that, and God, who makes everything work together, will work you into his most excellent harmonies.

Philippians 4:8–9

I have read this passage many times before, and in many versions, but this time it was different. I felt as though God was covering my weakness with His Word and filling me with His strength. I read the passage over and over and found myself drawn deeper into the revelation of Jesus Himself. I was struck by the fact that Jesus is true, noble and reputable. He is authentic—the real thing! He is not a copycat or a wannabe. He is not trying to be someone else. Jesus is authentically Himself; He is the Perfect One. Jesus is gracious and compelling. Another word for *compelling* is *undeniable*. Isn't that amazing?

This version of my favorite passage says to let your mind dwell on "the best, not the worst." It was here that I found myself getting tripped up. I would start strong, but soon I would let little things creep into my heart. My mind would begin to wander, allowing my thoughts to create pictures like those in a children's coloring book. Only the pictures were unpleasant, and then my imagination would kick in and begin to fill in a negative picture with vibrant color. I can see it so clearly now—a negative thought here and a destructive thought there, and soon the monster of misery would rise out of the basement of my imagination and rip the door of hope off its hinges. Of course, with my plumb line of peace destroyed, fear would move in and distort my view of God's personhood and His incredible power toward me, all while trying to rob me of my daughterhood in Him.

But God wasn't done with me yet. He summoned me to read my favorite passage again, while reminding me that the only way out was deeper in. I reread the verses more intentionally this time: "Summing it all up, friends, I'd say you'll do best by filling your minds and meditating on things true, noble, reputable, authentic, compelling, gracious—the best, not the worst; *the beautiful, not the ugly*" (emphasis added).

There it was again, that *beautiful* word! I flashed back to the church service in Texas when I had received the "beautiful word," and I realized that there was more—more beauty to be discovered in God . . . in me . . . in everyone. I began to understand that all of us are on a Jesus journey, traveling down the radical road that is taking us from glory to glory. I could see now that He is our guiding light and our safe place in this crazy season of uncertainty . . . our peace in the midst of this storm.

It's Back

Over the next several weeks, my peace slowly returned. I came to understand that I had not lost my peace as a result of the virus; I had lost it because I forgot who I was in Christ! As I pressed deeper into the Scriptures, the beauty of my life in God was unveiled, especially through the apostle Paul's words: "For we are His workmanship, created in Christ Jesus for good works, which God prepared beforehand so that we would walk in them" (Ephesians 2:10).

The word *workmanship* in this passage is the Greek word *poiema*, from which we get our English word *poem*. Think about it: We are God's poem that He is writing to the world, the very revelation of His heart toward humanity. In fact, Paul also wrote, "You are our letter, written in our hearts, known and read by all men" (2 Corinthians 3:2).

> We are God's poem, His letter, His song ... not just a melody, but the color and depth that come from a song when the melody and harmony flow together, intertwined with passion and love.

We are God's poem, His letter, His song . . . not just a melody, but the color and depth that come from a song when the melody and harmony flow together, intertwined with passion and love. What a beautiful picture of our life in God. He is the Master Poet, and we are the poem He writes as His living words. I could see it all so clearly now. Our trials are like jars of ink into which He dips His pen to make a poem of our lives. Or they are like jars of paint that He uses as He gracefully dips the tip of His brush into the trials of our existence and creates a masterpiece on the canvas of our life.

The more I pondered my position in Christ, the more I came to understand that His work in me was supposed to flow through me, to those around me. I cannot hoard God's beauty and the reassuring peace that ensues from it for myself. No way! I am a giver, His poem that must be shouted aloud to the hurting and the fearful. I am beautiful in God, but like Queen Esther, my beauty is for a purpose: that others would experience His reassuring peace and the revelation of their nature in Jesus. You, too, are beautiful, and He wants you to *"be you, till you're full"* of everything He has placed in your heart.

I Wish I Were You

Oh sure, there are always things about us we would like to change. That's just human nature. But when we step beyond the area of petty dislikes about ourselves, we enter into territory that becomes very dangerous. Yes, it is subtle at first. *I wish my eyes were green instead of brown. I think my nose is too long, and I like Jackie's better. I wish I had Sue's metabolism. She can eat anything she wants and never gain an ounce.*

But it does not stop there. We start doing the comparison game, and when we play that game, we never win. It is kind of like putting a frog in a pot of cold water and then turning up the heat slowly. The frog never sees what's coming and ends up being boiled alive. If he had known his outcome, you can bet he would have jumped out as fast as he went in.

> Riding on the what-if train is not going to get us anywhere except in trouble.

Riding on the what-if train is not going to get us anywhere except in trouble. What we are really saying is, *God made some mistakes when He created me, and I don't like them.* The enemy highlights a small blemish, and we turn it into a huge abscess. What may have deserved a moment of our time or attention has now turned into a lifestyle—a lifestyle of self-hatred and destruction. It is no wonder suicide is so rampant among our young people.

I want to challenge you to destroy the old film of yourself. Take your negatives and turn them into positives. In the early years of Bethel School of Supernatural Ministry (BSSM), we took our students on a retreat to the N.E.D. camp in Whiskeytown, California. It's a beautiful eighteen-cabin camp facility owned by the National Park Service. Each year, many middle schoolers spend a week at the camp to learn about their environment. The camp is a mixed forest of manzanita, pine and oak, and nearby are canyons full of tall ferns, freshwater ponds and lots of wildlife. During the off-season, we could rent the camp to hold our own BSSM retreat. The camp became something we looked forward to visiting year after year, and our ministry students and staff alike all felt God's peace there.

One particular year, I was spending time with a gal to help walk her through some things. After listening to her story, I could see that she felt stuck. The Lord showed me a picture that helped her get a breakthrough. At the time, I was into photography, and I saw a strip of negative film. I shared with her what the Lord was showing me, and at the very end I said, "When you hold a 'negative' up to the light, it can't be reproduced."

Just then, a light came on in her brain and she understood that she had power over her situation because she could change the way she saw herself. She could hold her "negatives" up to God's revealing light and get rid of the power they held over her. She was not a loser; she was a winner, with a purpose and a destiny. She was called and equipped to touch people in ways that only she could do.

Finding Your Place

So much of feeling "beautiful" or having confidence in my personhood is finding my place in the Body of Christ. I love how Paul explains it in Romans 12:3–6, especially in the Message Bible. It is such a great reminder of who we are and what we were created to do:

> The only accurate way to understand ourselves is by what God is and by what he does for us, not by what we are and what we do for him.
>
> In this way we are like the various parts of a human body. Each part gets its meaning from the body as a whole, not the other way

around. The body we're talking about is Christ's body of chosen people. Each of us finds our meaning and function as a part of his body. But as a chopped-off finger or cut-off toe we wouldn't amount to much, would we? So since we find ourselves fashioned into all these excellently formed and marvelously functioning parts in Christ's body, let's just go ahead and be what we were made to be, without enviously or pridefully comparing ourselves with each other, or trying to be something we aren't.

There is a place in the Body that only I can fill. When I find my place and fill that space with who I am in God, I become like a diamond put in its setting, which brings out the best in me. In turn, I bring out the best in those around me. The challenge comes when there is a season change and my previous mission is accomplished or nearly complete. I may be a "beautiful" diamond, but I can begin to feel purposeless until I find my new setting and understand my new mission.

> I felt like a fish out of water. In the beginning I saw Kris as the pastor, and I saw myself as the baggage that came along.

This was exactly what happened to me several years ago when I found myself in the middle of an identity reset. Ever since Kris and I had been married, I had always worked in a "man's world." Even in our parts stores, most of the employees were men and I knew my place on the team. I didn't feel the need to turn a wrench or change the oil in a car. Yet it helped that I had been raised by a father who was in the automotive business, so this was nothing new to me. Kris did his thing and I did mine, and seldom did our responsibilities overlap, which made for a great working relationship for both of us.

But when we moved to Redding and began working at Bethel, I felt like a fish out of water. In the beginning I saw Kris as the pastor, and I

166

saw myself as the baggage that came along. My identity felt as if it had been ripped away from me, and I was hanging on to anything I could get my hands around. Kris knew the Bible really well, and I didn't. He was a great speaker, and I wasn't. Kris was really wise in his counsel, and I was afraid that I wouldn't have anything to say if I was ever put into a situation where I had to talk someone through a tough situation.

I began to think of people whom I admired and who had everything going for them. *If I could just be like Kris*, I thought, *or if I could just be like Heidi Baker, a woman who is full of power and loves people, I would feel as though my life had some meaning. If I could just be bolder and more outgoing, I would have more opportunities for ministry coming my way.* Sadly, the comparisons just kept on coming, which sent me into a state of despair. I was experiencing many of the same insecurities I have had through the years, but this time they were rooted in losing my accustomed place through our transition and missing my purpose. Something needed to change.

Remembering the Monuments

When Joshua led the Israelites across the Jordan River on dry ground, God commanded him to set up stones there that would be a memorial to remind them of God's works in their lives (see Joshua 4:1–9). So I decided that in the midst of losing my place in life, I would purposely recall to my mind other times of transition that had occurred for me. This exercise in remembering would reassure me that I would again find a new and better place in our new life in the near future.

I sat myself down and began thinking of my life over the past forty years. I started by recounting all the things I had accomplished. At the age of 11, I was recruited by the Oakland Raiders football team to twirl baton as a Raiderette. At 15, I purchased my very first car, a brand-new Datsun B-210 straight off the showroom floor. I had been saving my money for years, and my parents loaned me the rest of the funds I needed for my down payment. Of course, I couldn't get a loan from a bank at that age, but my dad took one out in his name. I made payments on the car for two more years, until I paid the loan off in full. On the day I turned 16, I landed my first job as a server in a local steakhouse. Yet the one thing I wanted most of all was to be married. Finally, my parents consented to allow me to get married at 17, as long as I first graduated from high school. I had found a way that I could attend extra classes each day and graduate in three years instead of four, all while participating in a two-year biomedical program offered through UC Berkeley for students interested in going into the medical field. I graduated from high school at 17 and married Kris the very next month. When I was 18, Kris and I purchased our very first house. By the time I was 22, I had given birth to three of my kids. We opened up our first business when I was 24, and at the age of 40 I became a grandmother.

Though I might not have ever had input into the lives of the presidents of different nations around the world the way my husband has, I have taken part in shaping the lives of many young kids in children's church, which I led for over nineteen years. I have extended a glass of cold water to many demon-possessed people, and I have invited them into my home and helped them find freedom and wholeness. In our auto parts stores, I have counseled more men sitting across the counter than I ever have on a Sunday morning in church. Most of those men would never, ever step foot inside a church, but they poured their guts out to me.

It was not long before the exercise of revisiting my monuments led me to a renewed confidence in my soul, which resulted in being able to find my place of purpose and meaning both at Bethel Church and at BSSM. Soon I was thriving again, as I have all my life. Together, Kris and I were building the school of ministry, seeing hundreds of people get set free and training revivalists from all over the world at BSSM, teaching them what we had learned in our "little house on the prairie" days.

Finding Myself in Weakness

Despite the challenges we faced in our earlier years, I've had a pretty great life. Actually, I've had more than a great life! I am amazed at the many different things I have accomplished in my lifetime, with the help of the Lord. I have been in great health and have even taken pride in my ability to do almost anything I put my mind to. But in 2015, I began to notice things happening in my body. My arm began to "ratchet" when I would move it. I remember thinking that it was just muscle strain, and I didn't even share the symptom with Kris.

Working with my horses every day had made it easy to rationalize that the ratcheting movement was due to a pulled tendon or another injury. But after months of dealing with it, I realized that it was probably more than just a strained muscle. I began taking ibuprofen and doing stretching exercises during the day, hoping those would help. Nothing seemed to make a difference.

About a year later, I noticed that my hand was beginning to shake. That created some concern in my heart. I went to the doctor, who said it was probably just a benign tremor. This went on for another year and my symptoms got worse, so I went back to the doctor for another exam. The doctor recommended that I go see a specialist more equipped to deal with my issue.

I made an appointment for an examination with a neurologist in a city not far away. He had me perform different movements with my body, and he asked me a series of questions. When it was all over, he sat me down and said, "You have Parkinson's."

I suddenly felt as if my world had caved in and I was being suffocated with the truth. I remember not knowing what to ask this neurologist.

It was as if my mind couldn't comprehend what I was hearing. He told me that there was no definitive test to confirm Parkinson's, but that the diagnosis was based on my symptoms.

I left his office with a flood of emotions going through me. I prayed that this was just a bad dream and that I would wake up from it at any moment. My mind was flooded with questions: *What's going to happen to me? What am I going to do? What will I be unable to do?* I had no answers for any of them. I had always been such an active person, one who could do anything I set my mind to. I would never say never to anything. Now, I was being faced with this challenge that questioned my beliefs.

That was years ago, however. As of the writing of this book, although I have had to change some of the ways that I do life, all in all it has worked out fine. I have come to the place where I have accepted the fact that I get tired more easily and sometimes I have to lie down and take a nap. The big *S* (for *Superwoman*) on my chest has shrunk a bit, and I have to let others do some things that I always did for myself. It is important for me to stay active, working my muscles as much as I can. I not only continue to ride horses, but I also went on my first hunting trip to Texas with my son and granddaughter. I just bought a bass boat, and I fly-fish on the weekends with Jason.

> I have chosen to move ahead and modify the way I do life a bit, but I haven't stopped living. I give myself a bunch of grace.

Kris has been extremely supportive, and he is always encouraging me. He never makes me feel as if I am failing because I can't do as much as I used to. I have chosen to move ahead and modify the way I do life a bit, but I haven't stopped living. I give myself a bunch of grace, realizing that I'm not 30 years old anymore and it's okay if I don't act like it.

Unfortunately for me, it has taken me 63 years to realize that I can relax and just be me. I understand now that I have been my own worst enemy, pushing myself to compete against myself in a way that has been unhealthy. Life is not a trophy to be won; it is a journey to be enjoyed.

My memories have often taken me back in time, to remembering the moment when Kris and I were standing under a tall oak tree at our favorite campground, carving our initials in the trunk: *KV + KT*. If I close my eyes, I can still taste the ice cream that we used to buy from the local ice-cream stand. Each night, we would walk out onto the pier, kick off our shoes and talk for hours about nothing that mattered.

That was so long ago. It makes you realize that you don't have time to waste, but you do have so many memories yet to make. It took some prodding from my husband and kids, but I decided that in this particular moment in time, doing something for me was just as important, if not more important, than doing something for others. I have always been great at serving others. I just haven't been great at taking time to do the things that I like to do, not to mention taking time to rest. Seasons change. Things don't stay the same, and that's how God intended our days to be. Don't get stuck living your life in the past. Welcome the new challenges and opportunities that are about to come into your future.

FIFTEEN

THE FINAL FRONTIER

Lord, your endless love stretches from one eternity to the
other, unbroken and unrelenting toward those who fear
you and those who bow facedown in awe before you. Your
faithfulness to keep every gracious promise you've made passes
from parents, to children, to grandchildren, and beyond.

PSALM 103:17 TPT

When you are accustomed to the sounds of your family surrounding you pretty much all of your waking days, their absence can be quite deafening. But just about the time you're done mourning the loss when your kids leave the nest, and you spend hours fasting and praying about how you're going to do life without them, they come back with a bunch more little munchkins in tow. I mean, how do you lose these people?

I am kidding, of course, but not about them coming back. They do return, often sooner than you think. When your adult children return home with their children, you wonder if you should enact revenge on them for all the things they did to you when they were kids. Or you wonder if you should lend an ear of empathy as they share their sorry stories of the struggles they are having with their own children. Then you consider that their sorry stories are virtually the same ones you had when *they* were kids, so you realize that God has vindicated you!

Of course, as grandparents we have a tremendous advantage over these newbie parents because we have been through it all before, so we have a pretty good idea about how it all ends. Now, however, it is time for our next great feat in life as we journey into the final frontier of child-raising—learning the role of grandparenting. Here's the deal: You know it is different than parenting, but you are not sure how.

> It is time for our next great feat in life as we journey into the final frontier of child-raising—learning the role of grandparenting.

In the early stages of having our grandkids, the transition toward this final frontier was quite complex for Kris and me. You spend eighteen or so years raising your kids, speaking into their lives and disciplining them when necessary. Then all of a sudden you realize that you are Grandpa and Grandma, not Mom and Dad. No longer are you the ones responsible for the little ones' everyday lives. That place has been given to their parents. I am not saying that as grandparents we don't have a place in our grandkids' lives. I am saying that our place looks different. Most of the time, you learn grandparenting the same way you learned parenting—a little bit, by hook and by crook, sometimes by watching others, and other times by overstepping your bounds.

I was not present with Kris when he learned that last lesson. Evidently, one afternoon Jason and the kids were over to the house and Elijah was goofing off, just trying to have some fun. He must have been around seven years old at the time. Jason told him to sit down, and

Elijah smarted off to his dad, turned and started to leave the room. Kris immediately jumped up and started to correct Elijah. Jason put his hand on his father's shoulder and said, "I've got this, Dad!"

Later that night, Kris and I were lying in bed, talking about what had transpired between Jay and him. "I think I overstepped my bounds," Kris recounted. "I was acting like Elijah's father instead of letting Jason handle the situation, so I think I owe Jay an apology. I never meant to undermine his authority."

"No, you didn't mean to do that," I said. "When you've been a parent for so long, it's just hard to step aside from that role and let someone else do it. It would be different if Elijah's parents were away and you or I were watching him. Then that place would be ours to take," I consoled.

> **I find that the best thing for me to do as a grandparent is to let my kids know that I'm here if they need me.**

I am glad that scenario happened to Kris first, because Jason's correction helped shape the role I take as Grandma. Since then, I have tried really hard not to offer my opinions when they are not asked for. Yet I have to say that sometimes it's really hard to bite your tongue. I find that the best thing for me to do as a grandparent is to let my kids know that I'm here if they need me. I had my turn raising kids; now it is my kids' turn. Of course, it becomes a problem when as a grandparent you think your grandchild is violating the laws of God, but at the same time the child's parents (your kids) are thinking that their little one throwing food at people in a restaurant from his or her high chair is rather charming. Ugh! But ultimately, it all sort of works out.

I Can't See!

One of the funniest Vallotton family stories happened years ago with our oldest grandson, Elijah. My son Jason received a phone call from

Elijah's after-school daycare center at Bethel. He could tell something was very wrong by the tone of the aide's voice who was calling.

"Jason, there's something very wrong with Elijah," the aide said. "He's complaining that he can't see, and he's beginning to freak out!"

"I'll be right there," Jason replied. As he arrived and entered the room, he could see Elijah sitting in a chair with his back toward him. "What's wrong, Elijah?" Jason inquired.

"I can't see, Dad! I can't see! Everything's so blurry," Elijah cried. "I'm so scared!"

"I'm going to take you to the emergency room right now. There may be something wrong inside your head that's causing your blurry vision. Can you walk okay, son?" Jason asked.

"I think so," Elijah whimpered.

"Hold on to my arm and I'll guide you," Jay said as they began to leave the classroom. They needed to navigate a long flight of stairs in order to reach the lower level. "Can you make it?" Jason questioned.

"I don't know, Dad," Elijah said. They took each step slowly, but Elijah tripped several times, gasping with fright and clinging to the side rail as if his life depended on it.

"I'm going to call the doctor to see what he suggests," Jason explained. He made the call and the phone rang, and soon the familiar voice of our doctor was on the line. Trying not to sound frantic, Jason explained Elijah's symptoms the best he could.

"You need to take him to the ER and get him checked out," our doctor told Jason. "They'll run some tests on him and be able to make a proper diagnosis."

"Thanks, Doc. I'll let you know what the ER says," Jay mumbled. He then warned his son, "Lij, you know that you may need to get a shot if you go to the hospital."

Elijah was terrified of shots and burst into tears. But he insisted, "I still can't see, Dad. It's getting really bad!"

It was a fifteen-minute ride to the hospital. Elijah sat quietly looking out the window, and then suddenly he exclaimed, "Dad, that looks like Dann Farrelly in the car next to us!"

"What do you mean, Elijah? I thought you couldn't see," Jason questioned.

"Well, uh, I mean I can see a figure that looks like Dann, and the color of that car looks like his," muttered Elijah. "I can hardly see at all right now."

"Are you sure?" Jay prodded.

"Why doesn't anyone believe me?" Elijah cried through sobs and tears.

"We're almost at the hospital. We'll figure out what's wrong with you," Jason reassured him. "Don't worry, buddy!"

It was about 5:30 in the afternoon by then. The guys walked into the ER with Elijah putting his hands out like a blind man so as not to run into anything. Once the paperwork was complete, Jason found a few empty seats and they sat down.

"Wow, Elijah," Jason said. "They're really busy tonight. We may be here for a while."

Around that time, I called Jay to see if he wanted something to eat.

"I would love that, Mom," Jay replied. "I haven't eaten all day."

I arrived at the hospital about an hour later with burgers and fries. There were so many people in the ER that Jason told me, "Mom, don't wait around. I'll let you know what the doctors say. Thanks for the food!"

I felt so bad for Elijah. He was so scared. The condition of the older lady sitting next to him was not helping any. She was hunched over in her chair, moaning and writhing in pain.

"Dad, do something for her. You've got to help her!" Elijah said in a panicked voice.

"What do you want me to do, Lij?" Jason questioned.

"I don't know! Maybe let her go see the doctor before I do," Elijah suggested.

"I can't do that, Lij. You may have something really wrong with your brain that needs immediate attention," Jay explained. "She's going to have to wait her turn."

Elijah looked as if he was going to throw up because there was so much pain and sickness all around him. Finally, he was taken back to an examination room. Jason shared Elijah's symptoms with the ER doctor, who then put Elijah through a series of tests.

"I need to order an eye pressure test, along with a CT scan of Elijah's brain," the doctor explained to Jason when he finished. "I want to make sure that we rule out a brain tumor."

Elijah was taken into another room, where they performed the tests. The doctor returned with Elijah in tow sometime later. He explained to Jason that the tests had come back negative.

"I can't find anything wrong with Elijah. However, I want you to take him to an optometrist in the morning," the doctor suggested.

By the time the guys left the hospital, it was after midnight. The next morning, Jason was able to get an emergency appointment with an optometrist. Upon their arrival, Jay was asked to fill out paperwork describing Elijah's symptoms and medical history. Jay filled out the form, and an assistant escorted the two into the examination room. The assistant performed several tests on Lij, asking him if he could read a lower row of letters that were small.

"I can't make them out at all," Elijah murmured.

"What about the next line up?" he asked, pointing to larger letters. They made their way up to the huge letters in the top rows, with Elijah becoming more and more frustrated along the way.

"I think I see a . . . um, it looks like a *Z, E, G* . . ." Finally, Lij just yelled out, "I don't know what the other letters are! Everything's blurry!"

The assistant was unsure what to do next. He pulled the equipment away from Elijah's eyes and went to get the doctor. After what seemed like an eternity to Elijah, the doctor walked into the exam room.

"Hi, Elijah!" the doctor said with a big smile on his face. "I hear that you're having some vision trouble. I want to have you finish reading this eye chart and tell me what the smallest line is that you can read."

Elijah, squinting with all his might, said that he could only see the very largest letter, but that it looked more like a spaceship than an actual letter.

"I think we're all done here," the optometrist said. "Why don't you go out to the front office and pick out a sucker? I want to discuss my findings with your father."

Feeling excited to make his escape, Elijah strolled down the hall to retrieve his sucker.

"There's absolutely nothing wrong with your son," the optometrist stated matter-of-factly to Jason. "Stress can cause kids to do some of the craziest things."

"My wife and I have just gone through a divorce, and it has been really hard on Lij. I'm really sorry for wasting your time, but I'm so thankful you were able to take us in so quickly," Jason explained with a weak smile.

As Jay left the doctor's office, he gathered up Elijah while trying to hold in the anger that was welling up inside him.

"When do I get my glasses?" Elijah inquired.

"The doctor said your eyes are fine and you don't need to wear glasses. I'm taking you back to school, and we'll talk about this later," Jay said in a stern voice.

"But I can't see the board at school," Lij cried.

"Then we'll move you up to the front row," Jason insisted, dropping Elijah off and heading back to work. He wanted to scream, but then he thought, *I don't know what to do, but my dad will know!*

179

The Wisdom of Experience

The phone rang, and Kris answered it. Jason recounted the day's events and how it had gone at the eye doctor's office. "I'm so angry, Dad! I don't know what to do," Jay blurted out.

"I think you need to take him back to the eyeglasses place and buy him a pair of glasses that have no magnification in the lenses," Kris said. "Let him pick out the frames and see if that fixes his problem."

"You've got to be kidding, Dad! That will just fuel the problem. I feel as if I'm giving in to his lying, and I don't know if I can do that," Jay pushed back.

"Trust me, son. I've been around this mountain more times than I can count," Kris said. "A child will do anything—positive or negative—to get attention."

Jason headed back to pick up Elijah and told him, "I've been thinking about your eyes, and I've decided that glasses will probably help you. Let's go pick out a pair and see."

> "Trust me, son. I've been around this mountain more times than I can count."

Elijah's mood perked up, and a huge smile filled his face. The guys arrived at the eyeglasses store, and Jason sent Elijah in to try on some frames.

"Is there something that I can help you with?" the salesperson said.

"There sure is. I need to buy a pair of glasses that have no magnification in the lenses," Jason stated.

"All our displays come with a non-magnification plastic lens," the salesperson said. "You choose the frame, and we'll fill the lens with your prescription."

"We won't be needing a prescription filled. The frame will do just fine," Jay explained. "Hey, buddy, what do you think about these glasses?" Jason showed Elijah an ugly pair of frames much too large for his face.

"Let me try them on," Elijah said. Looking at himself in the mirror while squinting his eyes, he said, "I can see better now, but let me see if there's another pair that helps me more."

Jason pulled out several more pairs of glasses, and then Elijah found a pair himself and said, "What about these, Dad?"

Jason looked at the frames and then at the price tag that read $400. He gasped. There was also a fairly large sticker that had the D&G logo plastered to the front lens, indicating that this was a more expensive designer frame.

"Let me try them on, Dad!" shrieked Elijah with excitement. "Oh, wow, Dad, I can see perfectly! These are the right glasses for me," Elijah said as he gawked at himself in the mirror.

Jason handed the frames to the salesperson and said he would like to purchase them.

"Do you have a script for the prescription?" asked the clerk.

"No, I just want to purchase the frames. He can see perfectly with this pair," Jay replied.

The clerk looked at Jason as though he were an idiot. "Okay, would you at least like me to take the initials off the lens?"

"No, leave them on!" cried Elijah as he grabbed the frames and put them on his face. "These are perfect!"

They left the store with Elijah "miraculously healed." Several days later, Jason went to school to pick up Elijah. As he walked into the room, there was another father picking up his son. Noticing Elijah's new glasses with the D&G logo on the lens, this father said, "Nice shades you have on!"

"I just got them, and I can see so much better now," Lij said with a cute grin.

"Those aren't real glasses," the father replied. "They're fake!"

"No they're not!" shouted Elijah. "They're real! Tell him, Dad! Tell him!"

Jason turned around and ushered Elijah through the door and down the hallway, wondering if the day was ever going to end.

Honesty above All

A few days later, Don Mayer, the principal of the Christian school the kids attended, called Jason and asked to meet with him. He had a concern about Lij. "I don't know if you're aware of this, but Elijah spent $60 on three T-shirts that he bought for a few of his friends. When I questioned him about the money, he said his grandmother had given it to him for Christmas. I'm not sure if the story is true or not, but I thought you'd want to know."

"Elijah," Jason called out as Elijah walked through the front door later. "Come over here and sit down. I have something I want to talk to you about. Mr. Mayer called me into his office today and said you bought three T-shirts for $60 and gave them to your friends. Is that true?"

"I did, Dad," Elijah confessed. "Grandma gave me the money at Christmas, and I've been saving it."

"You can't even go one week without spending a buck!" Jason said in frustration, knowing that Lij hadn't really saved any of his Christmas money. "You're lying to me, Lij, just as you did about your eyesight! Those lenses aren't real; they're just a piece of plastic. There it is: scientific proof that you being able to see had nothing to do with those glasses!"

Elijah tried his hardest to deny the accusations, but soon he burst into tears and threw his glasses across the room.

"Elijah, I will always love you no matter what. But you have to tell me the truth," Jay insisted.

As the story unfolded, it became clear what was motivating Elijah. One of the girls in Elijah's class had come to school with new glasses and had received a lot of attention. He thought that if he got glasses, too, he would get the same response. He also thought that if he did something nice for his friends, he would get even more attention.

"You know, Lij," Jason said, "you have a mess to clean up. I spent $400 on glasses when I didn't have the money to spend. You took money from Grandma, and then you lied to Mr. Mayer about it. Lij, lying is a very serious problem I see living in your heart. If you don't take the time to get to the root problem about why you are lying instead of telling the truth, it will follow you for the rest of your life. You also have a big mess to clean up with Mr. Mayer."

"I'll make it right, Dad," a repentant Elijah said after their talk. "I promise!"

> Elijah spent hours cleaning up manure and learning the meaning of "hard work." And to this day, Elijah is one of the most hardworking people we know.

Jason called Kris and relayed the events that had transpired over the last few days. "What do you think I should do, Dad? Should I just let it go, or what?"

"If I were you, Jay, I would make Elijah work off the money that he owes Grandma, as well as the $400 you spent on the frames. He needs to learn that his bad choices not only affect him, but also those around him," Kris instructed. "Dishonesty comes at a high price. This is a great opportunity for him to man up to his mistakes. He will never forget this week, I'm sure! I think I have the perfect place for him to work off his debt. My personal assistant, Nancy, has a goat farm, and I bet there's all kinds of manure lying around that he can scoop up. I'll give her a call and see if I can make it happen."

And so it did happen. Nancy was delighted to put Elijah to work, knowing that it would be a day he would never forget. Elijah spent hours cleaning up manure and learning the meaning of "hard work." And to this day, Elijah is one of the most hardworking people we know. Many times, we've all sat around the dinner table and listened to Jason tell this story about the eyeglasses and the goats, and each time, we laugh and laugh until our eyes water and our bellies hurt.

Jason is not the first parent to face this kind of situation. Every family has its challenges. As I stated back in chapter 2, it takes a village to raise a child. I bet whoever came up with that statement had a bunch of kids. You may not know what to do in a parenting situation, especially one that involves bouts of anger, depression, stealing and the like in your children. But you probably do have someone you can turn to who has the wisdom of experience and will have the answer.

It is one thing for a child to be strong-willed, but to be defiant is unacceptable. If you feel as if you are in a place as a parent where you have done everything you know to do and it has failed, don't be afraid to seek outside advice and even professional help. Children are very sensitive to their surroundings, and that sensitivity can manifest in many different ways. Some children become introverted, while in the same situation others become uncontrollable and lash out at anything or anyone who puts pressure on them. It is vital that we help our kids and grandkids deal with the issues of life before they get out of hand.

Creating an Empowering Family Culture

We discovered firsthand the destructive effects a negative family culture was having on some of our grandkids as they were in the throes of trying to navigate their parents' divorce. In those days, we were trying hard to mitigate the painful effects of rejection and confusion in the hearts of our whole family. This caused us to wonder how we could proactively create a family culture that would not only neutralize the various manifestations of our painful situation, but that would also empower the Kingdom in the life of our family. I knew that to help bring out the best in each of us, we had to incorporate the strengths of the Vallotton family into whatever structure we developed.

In the midst of my contemplation about all of this, I made an encouraging discovery. When I was going through some files, I came across letters that Kris and I had written to our kids during the Christmas season of 1991. I had forgotten all about the letters and was so excited when I stumbled upon them. I felt as if I had just discovered a buried treasure chest. Sitting down, I started reading through each letter. I sensed that God was pulling me back into a time when the kids were being shaped and molded into the people God had created them to be. We had written a specific letter to each child, describing prophetically his or her life calling, purpose and destiny. As I pored over these letters, I found strands of gold tucked away in them, delicately intertwined throughout the print in the form of prophetic words captured on paper.

It has been nearly thirty years since we penned the words in those Christmas letters, and the Lord has brought many of them to pass. Now we see our kids raising kids of their own, and they will in turn be passing down their own family traditions to our grandkids. Then those grandkids will pass them down to their kids, whom we may never meet with our eyes, but who will carry the heart and spirit of the Vallotton family forever.

Our family has grown up so quickly, and life is so busy for everyone that it has been a bit difficult to perpetuate that empowering culture in our family as we have all grown older. One Sunday, Kris and I were talking about remedying the situation. After some thought, we decided to get everybody together after church for family dinner at a local restaurant. Not everyone was able to join us because some of them lived too far away, but at least it was a start.

"Do you have an agenda for this family dinner?" I asked Kris.

"Not really," he replied. "Our lives are just so busy that I was thinking it would be fun to have some family time together."

That day when we got together, the conversation around the table was light and fun. We told stories, caught up on life, joked around and teased each other a bunch. It wouldn't be a Vallotton gathering without the jesting! When the laughter subsided, we all got up and went our separate ways. Before leaving, however, our grandkids looked over at us and said almost in unison, "Thanks for the great afternoon! We'll have to do this again sometime!"

Blue Bloods

Soon we were getting together as a family nearly every Sunday. While the COVID-19 virus was still in full swing, we moved our family dinners to our house. I really like being all together in our home better than meeting in restaurants. Since then, our family dynamic has taken on many of the elements of the wildly successful TV show *Blue Bloods*. The show is based on a family of Catholic New York City cops, the Reagans. The father, played by Tom Selleck, is the New York City police commissioner. One of his sons is an NYPD detective, the other is an NYPD sergeant, and his daughter is an assistant district attorney. The grandfather is the former police commissioner. If you haven't seen the show, you can still probably predict what the family dinner dynamics look like. Every meal begins with a Catholic-style prayer, so the family includes God in their value system and often in their conversation. Most of the family members are in the crime-fighting business, so the discussion often centers around their jobs. They all have strong personalities, plus their kids and wives also join in on the conversation, which makes it all quite entertaining.

Our family dinners have a very similar feel, except that we're not a crime-fighting family. Instead, all of us are in ministry of some kind. Our patriarch, Kris, is not the police commissioner; he is the senior prophet of our Bethel movement, so our dinners always have a prophetic element to them. I'm not saying that Kris prophesies over everyone at dinner, but there is an inherent grace that flows through his life and manifests through all of us as we interact with one another.

Most of us are on staff at a church, and three of our grandkids are going to BSSM (Bethel School of Supernatural Ministry). Our daughter Shannon co-pastored Mountain Chapel for years with her husband, and she is now the principal and superintendent of Douglas City School. So rather than talking about the latest person who was arrested or the perp who was shot in an alley, we're talking a lot about life, the good things that went on throughout our week and the people we're ministering to. Our grandkids are becoming adults now, so they are trying to figure out life—

> **Our times together are awesome, and our family really honors Kris and me not because we demand it, but because they carry honor and respect in their hearts for us.**

meaning they always have funny stories about their crazy learning experiences. And did I mention that everyone offers them heaps of advice?

Kris is a big personality, and he thinks it is his job to keep everyone stirred up. (The man is crazy!) I love serving and hospitality, so together we make a great team. Our times together are awesome, and our family really honors Kris and me not because we demand it, but because they carry honor and respect in their hearts for us. They often ask for our wisdom and prophetic insight into their lives.

Some of the most valuable times we have shared as a family are when we all help walk one of our family members through a hard time. It's comforting to realize that "all hell" may be breaking loose around us, but our family will always stand together with us. A great example happened a few weeks ago, when one of our kids was going through an incredibly hard situation that was potentially life altering. Kris decided ahead of time that our family dinnertime would be spent encouraging this person around the table. He sent a quick text to the rest of us and asked every member of the family to bring an encouraging word for this person.

I have to tell you, that was one of the most profound family meetings I have ever been in. Several of our grandkids took the lead and ministered to our hurting family member. With tears flowing, they broke demonic stuff off of the person, prayed hope into this hurting one and prophesied a fantastic future over this family member. Several hours later our dinner ended, but nobody wanted to go home. Our hurting family member left our house soaring, realizing that God had the situation all worked out and everything was going to be fine.

Built to Last

Kris and I have worked hard all our lives. We love excellence and enjoy creating and building things together around the house. The joke around Bethel is, "I wonder what the Vallottons are building while they're on vacation this year?" The funny thing is that it's not Kris or me who gets much use out of what we've built. But for the rest of the family, we've created an Oasis Fun Center right at our house. Take your pick: You can choose volleyball, badminton, swimming, horseshoes, Ping-Pong, horseback riding, a basketball court or pickleball. We also put in a children's playground for the littles.

And did I mention that Kris has a man cave where the guys can hang out, complete with a big-screen TV with surround sound, all for watching sports while yelling at the screen? And there's more! We have every video game known to humankind, with two more big screens to play them on. (If you don't get exhausted just reading all the opportunities available at our fun center, you must be superhuman.)

Our entire goal in building all this is to be parents and grandparents whom our kids and grandkids want to be with, and to have a house where they want to spend their time. I probably don't have to tell you that they are here all the time, with their friends along, too. In fact, most of the time we have to make them go home at night.

One funny family story is that when our granddaughter Rilie was a young girl, she was outside with Kris, who was cleaning the pool. She looked up at him with her big brown eyes and curly blond hair that covered most of her face, and she proclaimed, "Papa, my daddy said that when you die, this whole place is going to be his!"

Kris chuckled and replied, "You tell your daddy that I'm going to be so old when I die that he won't be able to enjoy it!" The funny things kids pick up from their daddies!

The Why behind the What

Let me end here by leaving you with the five Vallotton core values that we purposely weave into all our family gatherings:

#1 Create *connection* so that everyone knows they have a place where they belong and a family where they fit in.

#2 Cultivate a culture of *encouragement* where everyone can come and be refreshed and renewed.

#3 Construct a *prophetic atmosphere* that discovers the gold in each family member and calls out his or her divine destiny.

#4 Nurture a *counsel of wisdom* where every member can come for insights and answers to the challenges he or she faces in life.

#5 Foster a palace of fun where people can laugh, tease one another and find great joy in each other. It is the joy of the Lord that is our strength. Furthermore, Solomon said, "A joyful heart is good medicine" (Proverbs 17:22), so may our homes be a pharmacy of fun!

SIXTEEN

LEAVING A LEGACY

A good man leaves an inheritance to his children's children.

PROVERBS 13:22

We have ten grandchildren, and I love the role we play in their lives, which is still unfolding as they get older. Yet there is another dynamic that transcends our relationship with them. It was revealed to us twenty years ago through an encounter Kris had with the Lord. He was lying on the floor of the Alabaster Prayer House on the Bethel campus, praying for our family, when he had this crazy experience. He had a vision in which he was taken one hundred years into the future.

"How did he know he was seeing one hundred years into the future?" you ask. I don't know, but welcome to life with Kris Vallotton! In the vision, Kris was inside a beautiful mansion or palace and was standing next to a very old man. The man was in a gorgeous front room with a beautiful stone fireplace that rose about thirty feet to the ceiling. The house was filled with people, as if it was a family reunion or maybe Thanksgiving. Everybody was casually interacting, as families often do. The women were talking in the kitchen, and the men were hanging out in the front room. Several children played outside.

The elderly man was surrounded by several more young children. He was doing what old men do, telling stories and musing about the past. In the vision, Kris was standing right next to this elderly gentleman and could see him perfectly, but the man could not see him. The children were barely paying attention to the old man, until something happened to him. Suddenly, his countenance changed and he stared off into space, as if he was perceiving something divine, something profound. Then the tone of his voice changed as he started to recount the story of their royal family history.

Immediately, as if given a divine cue, the entire family moved with a sense of urgency toward the front room where the elderly man was sharing. They encircled him and sat quietly, listening intently to his every word as he recounted to them the history of their royal lineage, their divine prosperity and their God-given favor. Then he looked up at the fireplace, motioning with his hand, and he said, "And all of this began with your great-great-grandmother and great-great-grandfather."

> "From this day forward, you will live for a generation that you will never see."

Kris looked up, and above the mantle was a huge portrait of Kris and me! A moment later, Kris was back in the prayer house in a puddle of tears. Immediately, the Lord spoke to him and said, *You are no longer to live for a ministry—you are to live to leave a legacy! Your children's children's children are depending on you leaving them a world in revival. From this day forward, you will live for a generation that you will never see. You are to have a one-hundred-year vision so that you can build from the future.*

A Defining Moment

Kris got up off the floor that day a changed man. His entire motivation for life was transformed. Later that morning, Kris recounted the vision to me in tears. I knew this was a defining moment in our family, but I never imagined how big an impact this would have on us. This was more than a revelation; it was a mandate from God that was to become our family mission, our own royal lineage and the Vallotton legacy. This vision of our future helped us develop a strategy to apprehend God's goals for our lives. Consequently, from that day on, we began to build *from the future*, as the Lord had said.

Kris doesn't know how to ease into anything or transition incrementally into life changes. Oh no! He has to go BIG or go home!

One thing you need to know about Kris is that he doesn't know how to ease into anything or transition incrementally into life changes. Oh no! He has to go BIG or go home! So the next few years were like climbing Mount Everest with a man possessed with getting to the top. I caught the vision right away, but this was the time period when things were really tight for us financially, as I described earlier. At that time, we still owed over one million dollars and we were living hand to mouth. Bethel was paying each of us only a part-time salary at that point, so we didn't have anything extra, to say the least.

Consequently, I was all for building a strategic plan to leave a legacy, but I certainly wasn't ready to do anything practical yet, at least not financially. But it happened that one day soon after his encounter, Kris read a passage out of the book of Proverbs that fueled his passion: "A good man leaves an inheritance to his children's children" (Proverbs 13:22).

By now, you probably know where this is going. Kris insisted that we put $50 a month into a savings account at our bank for each of our grandchildren, and he wanted it to be set up as an automatic withdrawal so we wouldn't forget. You have to understand that this was radical generosity since we didn't have the money! Yet Kris had great faith that the Lord would provide the money because He had given him the vision. As Kris says, "God is Pro-vision. . . . He provides for His vision."

You should know that Kris really respects my opinion, and we always make important decisions together. We are committed to lead together, empowering each other in the places of our strengths. That being said, we also have a core value that enables each of us individually to obey the Lord's directives in our personal life, as well as in our family life. It really comes down to the fact that Kris and I trust each other's relationship with the Lord. Although I live with a man who has a radical personality, I also understand that he is a prophet who carries the responsibility to act on the voice of God in his life. He certainly has made mistakes in his walk with God, but not very often, so he has a great track record of leading us well. Consequently, when he told me what he wanted to do, I opened a savings account for the grandkids and set up the automatic withdrawals. From that day to this day, we have never missed a payment! That was more than fifteen years ago, and that money has enabled us to buy each of our grandkids his or her first car. We are also helping them with their education.

More Than Money

I want to share with you some of the things I've learned over the years from Kris's interactions with me and from his preaching. Kris taught me that a legacy is so much more than money or possessions. The most important part of a legacy has almost nothing to do with money. Moses put it this way: "The secret things belong to the LORD our God, but the things revealed belong to us and to our sons forever" (Deuteronomy 29:29).

So much of wealth in the Spirit is inherited. Think of it as "AirDropping" what you yourself have won in God to your children spirit-to-spirit. This principle is all over the Bible. Here is a great example: "Now Joshua the son of Nun was filled with the spirit of wisdom, for Moses had laid his hands on him" (Deuteronomy 34:9). Joshua's wisdom was the result of impartation, not experience, education or intelligence.

> **The most important part of a legacy has almost nothing to do with money.... So much of wealth in the Spirit is inherited.**

Much like Moses with Joshua, the apostle Paul had a spiritual son named Timothy. Paul often wrote as both a leader and a spiritual father to instruct Timothy. Here is a line from one of Paul's letters that gives us insight into his life: "Do not neglect the spiritual gift within you, which was bestowed on you through prophetic utterance with the laying on of hands by the presbytery" (1 Timothy 4:14). Leaders were AirDropping spiritual gifts to people, and the people were expected to receive the gifts and grow them for the benefit of others. We have often practiced this with our children and grandchildren. In fact, several of our family members operate in the same gifts that Kris and I have.

So many stories throughout Scripture are just as powerful as these, but the gifts in them are more caught than taught. For instance, you may remember the tale of Joseph, who was sold into slavery by his brothers, but who finally wound up interpreting a dream for the pharaoh of Egypt. Ultimately, Joseph's interpretation saved the nation and elevated Joseph to the number-two position of power over the entire country. How did Joseph learn to interpret dreams? Did he read Kris's *Basic Training for the Prophetic Ministry* manual or go through his *School of the Prophets* curriculum kit? Nah! It was in his family DNA, passed down from generation to generation as a legacy received through inheritance. Joseph's father, Jacob, was a dreamer and understood the language of the Spirit. Jacob's father, Isaac, was also a dreamer and had several encounters with God. Isaac was the son of Abraham and Sarah, so one or both of his parents had dreams, visions and even face-to-face encounters with God.

I hope you are catching this. Our relationship with God has inheritable qualities that we are to pass on to our children's children's children! Incidentally, two of our grandchildren are dreamers, and the Lord often speaks to them as He did to Joseph. We have really encouraged them to cultivate this gift and use it to help others.

More Than Gifts

Yet a legacy is also more than inheriting different abilities. A legacy actually creates favor with God. Are you asking, "What the heck are you talking about, Kathy?" Let me illustrate with a simple version of a complex story. A guy named Abijam became the king of Judah, and he was wicked and followed after other gods. But instead of God punishing Abijam for what he did wrong, God blessed him because of his father, David, who was righteous (see 1 Kings 15:1–5).

What is noteworthy here is that King David died 48 years before King Abijam was ever born! Abijam was the son of Rehoboam, who was the son of Solomon, who was the son of David. It is therefore clear that David's relationship with God was benefiting his great-grandchildren, in this case a family member whom he had never met. This is our heart—that our righteous relationships with God would benefit a generation that we won't meet until we get to heaven.

Speaking of kings who benefited from David's relationship with God, check out King Josiah. Here is the account:

Josiah was eight years old when he became king, and he reigned thirty-one years in Jerusalem; and his mother's name was Jedidah the daughter of Adaiah of Bozkath. He did right in the sight of the LORD and walked in all the way of his father David, nor did he turn aside to the right or to the left.

2 Kings 22:1–2

Josiah was born 322 years after King David died. Josiah's grandfather was Manasseh, who reigned 55 years in Judah and was the most wicked king in the history of Judah (see 2 Kings 21:1). Josiah's father was Amon, who reigned for only two years in Judah and walked in all the wicked ways of his father, Manasseh (see verse 19).

In other words, Josiah had some pretty powerful generational curses working against him, to say the least. But did you notice that the Bible does not name Manasseh or Amon as his father? Scripture names King David as Josiah's father. Beyond any biological lineage that may have been involved, what's more important is that Josiah tapped into the righteous root of King David by faith, who was himself king of the united kingdom of both Israel and Judah years earlier.

"Kathy, where are you going with all of this?" you ask. I am saying that our lives have an impact on others long after we pass through the veil called death. Because we are eternal beings, death is only the on-ramp to another dimension of life. Whenever we win a personal victory with God, who is eternal, we therefore create a covering for those people who are connected to our roots in God. This is the nature of inheritance, and it is part of our eternal reward and the privilege we have as joint heirs of Christ.

User-Friendly Eternity

I love Kris's theological revelation about living to leave a legacy; it is part of the benefit of living with a prophet. Of course, sometimes Kris comes out of his prayer time with ideas I have to hear over and over before I get them. But let me summarize some of the revelation about leaving a legacy that I have received as a beneficiary of being the wife of a prophet:

- God wants us to live in a way that helps the generations after us thrive.
- God literally wants us to be mindful of the impact we are having in the here-and-now on the then-and-there of those generations yet to be born.
- When we live with eternity in mind, we build a legacy, along with those who went before us, that will include those who are with us and those who will come after us.

I want to encourage you that you don't have to be a well-known speaker or live with a prophet or have a public ministry in order to leave an inheritance to your children's children. Nor is it necessary to have been raised in a Christian home in order to have a powerful impact on the generations to come.

Neither Kris nor I was brought up in a godly environment. We both saw plenty of the ugly in life before we made our way to the God and the good. So you can see from our lives and family that it is never too late to build a friendship with Jesus that will benefit everyone you love. I want to challenge you, therefore, to dare to dream, to live on the edge (of your faith) and to keep God in the center of it all!

Kathy Vallotton is a senior leader at Bethel Church in Redding, California, and has been part of Bill Johnson's apostolic team for over forty years. She and her husband, Kris, are the co-founders of Bethel School of Supernatural Ministry (BSSM), which has grown to 2,500 full-time students from over 76 countries worldwide. Kathy is also the co-founder of Bethel School of Worship, as well as Moral Revolution.

Kris and Kathy are entrepreneurial pioneers who have owned nine businesses, seven of those in the automotive field. Together, they direct KV Ministries and have traveled the world teaching and preaching about the goodness of God and the power of the Kingdom.

Kathy has a passion to see families and marriages restored, see the brokenhearted healed and see the oppressed set free. Kris and Kathy have been married for 45 years and have four children and ten grandchildren.

You May Also Like . . .

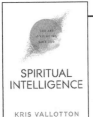

God invites us to bring our perspective into line with His—transforming our understanding and actually endowing us with spiritual intelligence. In this eye-opening book, Kris Vallotton explores how listening to the Holy Spirit and understanding what it means to have the mind of Christ gives us the capacity for life-transforming spiritual intelligence.

Spiritual Intelligence by Kris Vallotton
krisvallotton.com

Go deeper into the heart of one of the most crucial, compelling and controversial topics today: the office of prophet. In this definitive guide, Kris Vallotton offers foundational teaching and provides critical advanced training. You will come away empowered and equipped with the knowledge and skills needed for this vital supernatural ministry.

School of the Prophets by Kris Vallotton
krisvallotton.com

At this pivotal hour, when evil dominates the headlines and the media persecutes any dissenters, God is searching for men and women who will take a stand in His name. Even now, He is readying a heavy rain of revival. Here is the guidance you need to become a vessel that catches the downpour of the Spirit's rain—and helps release the Kingdom like a flood.

Heavy Rain, revised and updated edition by Kris Vallotton
krisvallotton.com

✅ Chosen

 Stay up to date on your favorite books and authors with our free e-newsletters. Sign up today at chosenbooks.com.

 facebook.com/chosenbooks

 @Chosen_Books

 @chosen_books

More from Chosen Books

Amid grueling personal circumstances, Jason Vallotton found himself stunned with grief and a sense of betrayal. Using his story as a poignant illustration of God's grace and healing, Jason invites you to reframe your own understanding of pain in terms of redemption, and discover a restored, fulfilled and powerful life!

Winning the War Within by Jason Vallotton with Kris Vallotton
jasonvallotton.com

God's crowning creation in the Garden was woman. Yet the state of our world belies her true beauty and purpose. In this compelling book, Kris Vallotton reveals God's true plan and purpose for all women—both in the Church and throughout creation. As sons and daughters of the King, it's time for men and women to work together to restore God's original design for biblical partnership.

Fashioned to Reign by Kris Vallotton
krisvallotton.com

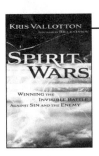

Sharing his deeply personal story of demonic bondage, torment and ultimate deliverance, Kris Vallotton turns the idea of spiritual warfare as we know it on its head. He reveals the diabolical lies and strategies of the enemy and arms you with a bold new battle plan. Now you can win the invisible battle against sin and the enemy. Victory is within your grasp. Will you take hold?

Spirit Wars by Kris Vallotton
krisvallotton.com